Abel H. Manoukian
The Deaconesses of the Armenian Church

STUDIA OECUMENICA FRIBURGENSIA

Published by the Institute for Ecumenical Studies
University of Fribourg Switzerland

113

Abel H. Manoukian

The Deaconesses of the Armenian Church

Translated by
David Zakarian

Aschendorff
Verlag

Münster
2024

Published with the support of the University Council (Hochschulrat)
of the University of Fribourg in Switzerland

With gratitude to the kind support of
Mr. and Mrs. Vasken and Haigo Kaltakdjian
to promote studies in Ecclesiastical History

Book cover: see p. 57.
Satz: Institut für Ökumenische Studien der Universität Freiburg Schweiz

© 2024 Aschendorff Verlag GmbH & Co. KG, Münster

www.aschendorff-buchverlag.de

ISBN (Print): 978-3-402-12276-1
ISBN (E-Book, PDF): 978-3-402-12277-8
DOI: 10-17438/978-3-402-12277-8

Table of Contents

Acknowledgements

The relationships between a man and a woman are nurtured through mutual love, which finds its origin in Christ, the Head of the Church. Christ regarded women as equal creations of God, who were also afforded, like every male, the same opportunities to approach God's word and redemption. The Church history, nevertheless, demonstrates that such a natural arrangement of equality between a man and a woman, as observed by its Founder, gradually weakened owing to the considerable pressure from the social relationships of the time, cultural beliefs, the influence of the milieu and the daily life, and especially because of the patriarchal morals. As a result, this arrangement lost its functionality, creating a hierarchical division of dominance and subordination between men and women in the church.

However, the Armenian Apostolic Holy Church, having engaged with the initial practice of the Early Church from ancient times to the present day, has preserved the custom of bestowing the rank of deaconesses on women, offering them a place in its hierarchical framework.

In the 1980s, I presented a concise paper entitled "Deaconess in the Tradition of the Armenian Church" at the Vienna State University's Department of Theology and History of the Eastern Churches. It was later published in a separate volume in 1991 in New York through the sponsorship of the Eastern Diocese of the Armenian Church of North America.[1] In 1994, the same volume was also published in New York in English, translated by Dr Prof. Peter Cowe, thanks to the St Nersess Seminary.[2]

This new volume is an updated version, with new bibliographical information and documentary photographs, which aims to corroborate that the tradition of deaconesses in the Armenian Church is one of the significant achievements of the Christian Armenian faith, the preservation and development of which should be one of the primary responsibilities of each Armenian believer and especially the episcopal order of our Church.

For the completion of this work, I particularly wish to thank everyone who encouraged me with their interest in the subject, specifically Dr Vahan

---

[1] Abēl Abeghay (a.k.a. Manoukian), *Hay ekeghets'u sarkawaguhinerĕ* (The Deaconesses of the Armenian Church), New York, 1991.

[2] A. Oghlukian (a.k.a. Manoukian), *The Deaconess in the Armenian Church: A Brief Survey*, trans. S. Peter Cowe, New York, 1994.

Ter-Ghevondyan, the former director of the Yerevan Mesrop Mashtots Matenadaran, and researchers – Dr Prof. Mane-Erna Shirinyan, Armine Melkonyan, Gayane Terzyan, and Dr Hratch Tchilingirian. Without their significant support, studying this material from different perspectives would have been impossible.

I also wish to convey my heartfelt gratitude to Dr. David Zakarian in Oxford for his exemplary translation of the present volume from both Western and Eastern Armenian originals into English, demonstrating unwavering diligence and precision.

May the ranks of the hallowed nuns and deaconesses mentioned in the present book intercede for all of us from their celestial heights, and may they blessedly keep this sacred and cherished tradition blooming in the bosom of the Armenian Apostolic Holy Church. With their angelic prayers, may they support the Armenian deaconesses' present and future missions, which are a gift to the Church.

Մի՛ ինչ նոր եւ անկարգ վարկցիս զայս, քանզի ի
սրբոյ առաքելոյն աւանդութենէ ուսանիմք, քանզի
ասէ՝ յանձն առնեմ ձեզ զՓիբէ քոյր մեր, որ է սպա-
սաւոր եկեղեցւոյն:

Մխիթար Գոշ

Do not regard this as something new and irregular,
because we have learned it from the tradition of the
holy apostle, since he says: "I entrust to you Phoebe our
sister, who is a servant of the church."[3]

Mkhit'ar Gosh

Preface

The position of women is quite controversial in the three largest monotheistic religions – Judaism, Christianity, and Islam. Women were commonly subordinated to men and were often excluded from participating in ritual, liturgical ceremonies. Even within Christianity, the journey of women towards equal rights continues. Even now, most Apostolic churches do not permit women's full participation in the hierarchical order, primarily invoking the church's two-thousand-year-old "tradition". However, the Christianity of the early period readily admitted that amongst the followers of Christ's movement, there could be women who, along with their brothers, were empowered by the grace of the Holy Spirit and were successful in making Christianity a worldwide religion by displaying eloquent testimonies of faith and earning their halos through the shedding of their blood in countless sacrifices of martyrdom.

Today, it does not constitute a miraculous phenomenon for a woman to assume the role of a country's president or prime minister or to lead nations, states, and major political and economic organisations and establishments. She can be an astronaut, conquer space, and travel many miles from Earth, but she cannot make a few steps in the church to ascend to the altar, to glorify God, and to communicate His holy and redemptive presence to the believers. This is a real issue, yet the response remains uncertain and the position of women within the church is currently unresolved.

---

3   Mkhit'ar Gosh, *Girk' Datastani* (Book of Judgement), edited by Khosrov T'oros-
     yan, Yerevan, 1975, p. 137; English translation by Robert W. Thomson, *Datasta-*
     nagirk' of Mxit'ar Goš, Amsterdam, 2000, p. 278.

Introduction

A few weeks ago, an acquaintance of mine sent me an email with the following enquiry:

> Along with the information about the Cheltenham parish, there is a photograph, where, standing on the altar, there are two *dpruhis*[4] (acolytes) next to the serving priest and two deacons. As per my knowledge, under the tenets of the Armenian Church, it is prohibited for women to ascend to the altar. Am I mistaken, or does what I have seen not apply to the Armenian Church?

The question related to a group photograph uploaded on the website of the US Eastern Diocese, which shows the altar of the Armenian Apostolic Church of the Holy Trinity in Cheltenham, Pennsylvania, in which the serving priest is standing with deacons to his right and left sides accompanied with two female acolytes dressed in church vestments and holding candlesticks. I am not aware of any responses that may have been provided by the other recipients of the letter mentioned above, however, one thing remained evident for me: there is an ambiguity concerning this matter in our Church. Are women really prohibited from ascending to the altar? If yes, then why? And if it is allowed in a general sense, then what traditional foundations or necessary grounds exist that have solidified this in the Armenian Church?

I will not speak about the stance of the Armenian Church on this issue, but I want to pose a question: is there a tradition by which women will be permitted to ascend to the altar to perform various liturgical acts?

Judaism, and in general, the Semitic culture, considered women unclean due to their menstrual period, hence not permitting them to approach or touch the Holy of Holies by ascending to the altar. Through the Old Testament, this custom had a particular influence on Christianity and became universally accepted by the nations which follow it. We should not forget that within the territories of the Roman Empire, the first converts were the Christianised Jewish communities, amongst whom not only the old Jewish beliefs and customs, but also the ritual operations were preserved. The Mosaic Law only permitted the tribe of Levi to approach the divine and assume the office

---

4 The term *dprhuri* is the feminine form of the noun *dpir* (acolyte), which designates an individual of the lowest rank within the church hierarchy, who engages in liturgical activities such as reading from the Bible and singing during the liturgy.

of the priesthood.[5] As a consequence of the old tradition, the right to preside a service by ascending to the altar is only given to someone explicitly chosen from among the men. The church confers on these men the offices of the diaconate, priesthood, and episcopate, initially by ordaining and then, at a later stage, also by bestowing upon them corresponding hierarchical authority through anointment. Thus, not only the lay population but women in general are prohibited from ascending to the altar.

The matter of women's ascent to the altar and their participation in liturgical ceremonies is closely related to the discourse on their involvement in the hierarchical order of the church. The question of ordaining women to the priesthood has presented itself as one of the most significant challenges of the church, spanning from olden times to the contemporary era. To this day, the Apostolic Churches do not permit women to be ordained or anointed as priests and to serve the church as equals to male priests in performing liturgical duties. As in the past, today, too, the Catholic, Orthodox, and ancient Eastern Christian Orthodox churches reserve this exclusively for men, each approaching the issue from their own perspective. History has, nevertheless, shown that in the early church, there were female disciples, prophetesses[6], virgins, widows, and deaconesses, who each played an active role in the organisation of the early Christian communities and made significant contributions to the spread of Christianity.[7] It was only in the Middle Ages that women, for some reason, were gradually deprived of assuming influential church offices.

The women's liberation movement, which commenced with the nineteenth-century French Revolution, has addressed, at different stages, the principles of equal rights between women and men. It was the church's obligation to respond adequately to these challenges that also arose among its members. If women stand out for various achievements in all spheres of life, be it economic, political, scientific, or cultural, then what is their rightful place and role in the church? What traditional structures are there to extend women's

---

5   See Dt 18:1-8 and Nm 1:49-53.

6   See Acts 21:8-9: "The next day we left and came to Caesarea; and we went into the house of Philip the evangelist, one of the seven, and stayed with him. He had four unmarried daughters who had the gift of prophecy."

7   For women's role in early Armenian Christianity, see David Zakarian, *Women, Too, Were Blessed: The Portrayal of Women in Early Christian Armenian Texts*, Leiden, 2021; Zaroui Pogossian, "Women at the Beginning of Christianity in Armenia", *Orientalia Christiana Periodica* 69, 2003, pp. 355-380; Joseph Blank, *Frauen in den Jesusüberlieferungen*, in: *Die Frau im Urchristentum*, ed. by Gerhard Dautzenberg, Helmut Merklein, Karlheinz Müller, Freiburg–Basel–Wien, 1989, pp. 9-91; Hans Küng, *Die Frau im Christentum*, Zürich, 2001, pp. 19-23.

sphere of activity, support their work dedicated to the church, make it more effective, and show genuine appreciation for it?

In response to the demands and the abovementioned challenges of the time, the Anglican, Old Catholic, and Protestant churches, particularly in recent decades, have begun to exhibit a discernibly favourable stance towards this matter. This not only to the question of priesthood but also through women's appointment to the episcopal rank to serve the church's needs on par with their male counterparts.

In contrast, the Armenian Church has followed long held customs, upheld a unique tradition from the life of the early Christian Church, and tried to maintain it, at least to some degree, to this day. Although women do not have authority to become priests, in our church, Armenian women have the right to assume the first office, alongside the episcopate and the priesthood, in the church hierarchy. This first ecclesiastical office, which springs from the essence of the church's mission of ministry and which was borrowed from ancient Greek into Armenian with its characteristic terms διάκονος and διακονία, is called *sarkawag* ("deacon") or *sarkawagut'yun* ("diaconate"): that is, it describes the special office of serving and assisting the Lord's church and His faithful flock.

Within our church, conferring the title of deaconess upon women is not a recent phenomenon. It is present in our church's history, and, albeit somewhat faded now, this tradition, still clearly emitting heartbeats and yearning for life, is a testament to the Armenian Church's appreciation of gender issues and its open-minded spirit. It also attests to her unbroken connection with the tradition of the ancient Christian Church.

Jesus and Women of His Time

Women did not play a significant role in society at the time of Jesus. Similar to certain cultures today, they avoided the company of men in public. Jewish sources from that period abound with negative descriptions of women. Men were advised not to speak much with their wives, let alone unfamiliar women. In society, women were supposed to live in isolation as much as possible. In the temple, they were permitted to gather and pray only in particular areas which were hidden from the male gaze; their status not dissimilar to that of slaves.[8]

It is noteworthy, however, that the Gospels display no constraints while describing Jesus' positive interactions with women, despite the possible inaccuracies in the biographic details they provide. In this regard, He clearly transcended all the restraints of contemporary social norms and customs, valuing in a woman her heart and soul, and her ability to follow God's Word and wanting to help her become His loyal and devoted follower. Not only was Christ's treatment of women not discriminatory, on the contrary, it was surprisingly non-restrictive and kind, entirely genial and unbiased. A group of devout women accompanied Him and His disciples from Galilee to Jerusalem while He preached and worked miracles in different places. They were also present at his crucifixion, after his burial and his glorious resurrection, when the disciples were in despair and some of them left the arena discouraged and returned home. Joanna, Susanna, Mary the Mother of God, Mary the wife of Clopas, the mother of James and Joseph, Salome, Mary and Martha of Bethany, as well as "many other women", and primarily Mary Magdalene, are all women commemorated in the New Testament. Jesus is not devoid of personal love and affection for women. Furthermore, the group of disciples who followed Christ, receiving no remuneration and lacking permanent dwelling places, was directly sustained by women and supportive families, including Mary and Martha of Bethany.

It is, of course, true that the closest circle of Jesus consisted of twelve male disciples, using the example of Israel's twelve tribes, but they were not called "apostles" yet. It was more than one generation after Jesus when the evangelist Luke identified the close circle of the twelve disciples as the "apostles".[9] The

---

8   Hans Küng, *Die Frau im Christentum*, loc. cit., p. 14.
9   Ibid., pp. 14-15.

truth is that the "apostles" sent to give good news of Jesus's glorious resurrection, were a much larger group, which undoubtedly included women such as the myrrh-bearers. Among them, the foremost was Mary Magdalene, who was destined to witness the first and the greatest grace.

In this respect, how mellifluous and precise is Mary Magdalen's characterisation given by the 13th–14th-century author and scholar Barsegh *vardapet*[10] Mashkeworts'i, who, in his commentary of the Gospel of Mark, described her as a person whom the Resurrected One directly "endowed with an apostolic title":

> And she wanted to approach and touch Him as she initially wished to, but He did not permit her, saying, Do not hold on to me"[11], for He will teach you that His body will not be the same as before death, but a celestial one and sublime. And although He did not permit [her] to approach, He, nevertheless, *endows her with an apostolic title*, saying: "Go to my brothers and say to them, 'I am ascending to my Father and your Father, to my God and your God'."[12] Having become worthy of these words, Mary comes and tells everything to the disciples. She will thus remain patient and benevolent. You, too, oh my beloved one, be patient, and you will become a *vardapet* and teacher for the students of the Word.[13]

---

10 In the Armenian Church, *vardapet* is an ecclesiastical degree which is awarded to celibate and learned priests after a rigorous course of study. The expression is synonymous with the Biblical term 'teacher' or 'master'.

11 John 20:17.

12 John 20:17.

13 Barsegh *vardapet* (Mashkeworts'i), *Meknut'iwn Srboy Awetaranin or ēst Markosi* (Commentary on the Holy Gospel by Mark), Vol. II, Constantinople, 1826, p. 427: Եւ ախորժէր մատչիլ եւ փարիլ ընդ նմա իբր յառաջագոյն՝ որպէս փափագէր, ուստի ոչ ետ թոյլ՝ ասելով, մի՛ մերձենար յիս, զի ուսուցէ թէ՝ ոչ եւս այնպէս իցէ մարմինն իւր՝ որպէս յառաջ քան զմահն. այլ երկնային եւ բարձրագոյն: Եւ թէպէտ յինքն մերձեալ ոչ ետ թոյլ, սակայն *առաքելական կոչմամբ պատուէ զնա*՝ ասելով. Ե՛րթ առ եղբարսն իմ եւ ասա գնոսա, ելանեմ եւ առ հայրն իմ եւ առ հայր ձեր, եւ Աստուածն իմ եւ Աստուած ձեր: Գայ Մարիամ՝ այսպիսի բանից արժանացեալ եւ պատմէ աշակերտացն. այսպէս իցէ ժուժկալել եւ մնալ բարլույն: Համբե՛ր եւ դու, ո՛վ սիրելի, եւ վարդապետ եւ ուսուցիչ լիցիս աշակերտաց բանիս: According to the subtitle of the published edition, the book is mistakenly attributed to the seventh-century Barsegh Chon, and sometimes to Barsegh Shnorhali. However, the author of the commentary on the Gospel of Mark is undoubtedly Barsegh Mashkeworts'i.

Evidence in the New Testament

When it comes to the bestowal of the rank of deacon upon women, significant evidence can be found in the verses Rom 16:1-2, 1 Tm 3:1, and 1 Tm 5:3-16.[14]

In his letter to the Romans, Apostle Paul called Phoebe *diakonos:* "I commend to you our sister Phoebe, a deacon of the church at Cenchreae."[15] Theologians have debated this matter, with some accepting the title and others expressing opposition. Some of them do not see any special religious meaning in the title of "servant" or "deacon" (Greek διάκονος) given by the Apostle, for in the early church, the concept of titles was clearly very vague, and the words *diakonos* or *diakonia* did not denote any specific service or ecclesiastical title.

Others, on the other hand, relying on the first verse of the first chapter of the letter to the Philippians, in which the Apostle greets deacons alongside all local Christians and bishops, conclude that in the ancient apostolic church at this time, the term *diakonos* clearly denoted a specific title within the ecclesiastical structure. As the feminine form of the word διακόνισσα = *diakonissa* = deaconess was not known at this time, it is likely that the precise use of the masculine form of the word by the Apostle also implied a reference to female deaconesses.

It can also be argued that in 1 Tm 3:11, "Women[16] likewise must be serious, not slanderers, but temperate, faithful in all things," Apostle Paul might be providing counsel to deaconesses, because this quote appears in the section that contains comprehensive instructions to deacons.

The general understanding of scholars of the subject is that the above-mentioned passage is addressed to deaconesses, although they did not yet have the ecclesiastical rank as it would come to be understood in later times.

---

14 In the letter to the Philippians, we should not dismiss the possibility that Euodia and Syntyche mentioned by the Apostle might have been deaconesses serving the local community: "I urge Euodia and I urge Syntyche to be of the same mind in the Lord" (Phil 4:2). Regarding deaconesses, also see the following study: Arat, Mari Kristin, „Die Diakonissen der armenischen Kirche aus kanonischer Sicht", *Handēs Amsōreay*, 1-12, 1987, pp. 153-190.

15 Rom 16:1.

16 The Classical Armenian text has "their [i.e. deacons'] wives".

The third reference to the deaconesses in the New Testament is found in 1 Tm 5:3-16. Here, the discussion revolves around the institution of *widowhood* and the responsibilities of a widow. The Apostle counsels against accepting young, widowed women "for when their sensual desires alienate them from Christ, they want to marry."[17] He advocates that the church should accept a widowed woman who fits the following description: "The real widow, left alone, has set her hope on God and continues in supplications and prayers night and day ... Let a widow be put on the list if she is not less than sixty years old and has been married only once; she must be well attested for her good works ...".[18] This expression "Let a widow be put on the list" suggests that there was indeed such a rank in the early church.

The entire tradition of the Eastern Christian Church and her brilliant representatives and patriarchs, such as Origen of Alexandria, John Chrysostom, and Clement of Alexandria, considered the three passages from the New Testament mentioned above to reflect the origins of women's diaconate.

Old and new icons of deaconess Phoebe, rendered in various artistic styles, have become commonplace in the Eastern Orthodox Churches. In this icon, the deaconess mentioned by the Apostle is presented in the church with the two main attributes of her service – the stole over her shoulder and the censer in her hand (likely originating from the mid-20th century).

---

17   1 Tm 5:11.
18   1 Tm 5:5-10.

Evidence in the First Three Centuries

Written work from the first three centuries of Christianity containing a direct reference to deaconesses has not reached us. From this period, pagan or Christian authors offer only indirect evidence that hints at the existence of deaconesses in the church, however their ecclesiastical rank is not clearly defined. In around 112 CE, in his letter to the emperor Trajan, the governor of Bithynia, Pliny the Younger, explained that he deemed it necessary to interrogate, using the method of torture, two slaves who are called "servant" = *ministrae* = *diakonos*, in order to learn the truth about their faith.[19]

Even though there appears to be a specific link between this information provided by Pliny the Younger and 1 Tm 3:11, it is impossible to determine the deaconesses' role in the church.

Ignatius of Antioch (d. 110 CE) wrote about "widows" who serve in the Church;[20] however, they, being virgins, differ from the widows described in 1 Tm 5.

Polycarp of Smyrna, who was a contemporary of Ignatius of Antioch, also addressed the responsibilities of widows and wrote that they ought to live a life befitting Christ, filled with prayers, and refrain from evil deeds, apostasy, and false testimonies because they are "the altar of God".[21]

These two examples, however, do not enable us to construct a distinct understanding of the role of deaconesses within the Church.

According to the information provided by Tertullian, widows belonged to the ecclesiastical class, but they did not hold any specific office and had no right to preach.[22]

---

19 Pliny, *C. Plini Caecili Secundi, Epistularum*, edited by Elmer Truesdell Merrill, Leipzig 1922, *300s.; Pliny, "C. Plinius ad Traianum, ep. XCVI, 8"*, in : Josephine Mayer (ed.), *Monumenta de viduis diaconissis virginibusque tractantia. Collegit notis et prolegomenis instruxit* (= Florilegium Patristicum), Vol. 42, Bonn, 1938, p. 5.

20 Translated from: "Die sieben Briefe des Ignatius von Antiochien," in: Franz Zeller (trans.), *Die Apostolischen Väter* (Bibliothek der Kirchenväter, 1. Reihe, Band 35) München, 1918, p. 154.

21 "Der Brief des Polykarp von Smyrna an die Gemeinde von Philippi", ibid., p. 165.

22 "Die zwei Bücher an seine Frau", in: Heinrich Kellner (trans.), *Tertullian, Private und katechetische Schriften*, Bibliothek der Kirchenväter, 1. Reihe, Band 7, München 1912, pp. 60-84.

Hippolytus, the Bishop of Rome, in his treatise *Traditio Apostolica* or "Apostolic Tradition," distinguishes widows from virgins by noting that the former were not ordained.[23] However, he does not acknowledge deaconesses in the modern sense of the term.

Clement of Alexandria (*ca* 150-215) and Origen (*ca* 185-215) also refer in their writings to widows who belonged to the ranks of the church but did not have the right to preach.[24] Even though both write about deaconesses, they, too, like all other authors of the second and third centuries, did not provide women with the authority to teach and perform rituals. In this period, the Church Fathers gave both widows and deaconesses instructions primarily related to a life of continence rather than any ecclesiastical authority in their communities.

---

23 Mayer, *Monumenta de viduis diaconissis virginibusque tractantia*, pp. 33-34; "Canones (Canones Hippolyti)", in: Valentin Gröne (trans.), *Tatian's, des Kirchenschriftstellers, Rede an die Griechen*, Bibliothek der Kirchenväter, 1. Serie, Band 28, Kempten, 1872, pp. 17, 41-43.

24 Clemens Alexandrinus, *Paedagogus* III, 12, 97; in: Mayer, *Monumenta de viduis diaconissis virginibusque tractantia*, p. 7; "Origines, In Isaiam hom." IV, 3, ibid., p. 8; "Origines, In Lucam hom." XVII, ibid., p. 9.

The Classical Period of Deaconesses (3ʳᵈ–6ᵗʰ cc.)

Syriac Didascalia Apostolorum or "Teaching of the Apostles"

In the discussion of deaconesses in his remarkable book *The Canon Law of the Armenian Church*, Nersēs *vardapet* Melikʻ-Tʻangean wrote,

> Deaconesses have existed since the time of the Apostle Paul (Rom 16:1); in the times of Justinian and Heraclius, there were 40 of them in the Church of Constantinople. The *Apostolic Constitutions* instructs that they should be forty-year-old virgins or pious widows. According to Canon XIX of Nicaea, they would receive a separate ordination. Their responsibilities included: 1) preparing women for baptism, 2) if the baptised were older women, they would perform the baptism, with the bishop or priest making the sealing of the covenant behind the curtain, 3) in the olden times they would be the god-mothers of baptised girls, 4) by the bishop's order they would be responsible for taking care of women, 5) [deaconesses] would stand near those church doors through which women entered and would ensure their orderly behaviour.[25]

It's important to remember that reliable sources about women in the diaconate reach us only after the third century and from sources produced in the Syriac milieu. The information above about deaconesses has been taken from the fourth-century collection of *Apostolic Constitutions*[26], composed in a Syriac-speaking milieu, which considered the Armenian Church, alongside other churches, not to be legitimate.[27]

The most significant source from this time is the Syriac *Didascalia Apostolorum*, edited in the mid-third century. This is an ecclesiastical treatise of the early Christian period. It was originally written in Greek, but its complete version has been preserved only in Syriac. This is the reason why it was often

---

25 Nersēs Melikʻ-Tʻangean, *Hayotsʻ ekeghetsʻakan irawunkʻě* (The Canon Law of the Armenian Church), Vol. II, Shushi, 1905, pp. 60-61.

26 This collection comprises eight chapters, with three of them (Chapter II, canon 58; Chapter III, canons 7, 15, and 16; Chapter VIII, canons 28 and 31) dedicated to discussing the rules on deaconesses.

27 See Nersēs Melikʻ-Tʻangean, *Hayotsʻ ekeghetsʻakan irawunkʻě* (The Canon Law of the Armenian Church), Vol. I, Shushi, 1903, pp. 56-66; H. Yakobos Tashean, *Vardapetutʻiwn Aṙakʻelotsʻ anvawerakan kanonatsʻ mateaně* (Didascalia Apostolorum: The Book of Unrecognised Canons), Vienna, 1896, pp. 78-82.

referred to as the "Syriac Teaching". This text was certainly influenced by *The Teaching of the Twelve Apostles* (Διδαχή των Δώδεκα Αποστόλων) and subsequently circulated attached to the *Apostolic Canons* as its section.

In the *Didascalia Apostolorum*, widows and deaconesses are clearly distinct from one another. A widow was a kind of secular ascetic within the congregation. She was forbidden from performing ritual services or preaching. The main responsibility of a widowed woman in the community was praying and caring for the sick. She was also permitted to carry out "ordinations", however, this does not imply the granting of ecclesiastical authority.

Deaconesses are mentioned alongside widows for the first time in Chapter XVI, "On the Appointment of Deacons and Deaconesses," of the *Didascalia Apostolorum*. Amongst various instructions to bishops regarding the performance of the baptism ceremony, we find a mention of the respective responsibilities of deaconesses, in cases where the involvement of male deacons was limited:

> Wherefore, O bishop, appoint thee workers of righteousness as helpers who may co-operate with thee unto salvation. Those that please thee out of all the people thou shalt choose and appoint as deacons: a man for the performance of the most things that are required, but a woman for the ministry of women. For there are houses whither thou canst not send a deacon to the women, on account of the heathen, but mayest send a deaconess. Also, because in many other matters the office of a woman deacon is required. In the first place, when women go down into the water, those who go down into the water ought to be anointed by a deaconess with the oil of anointing; and where there is no woman at hand, and especially no deaconess, he who baptizes must of necessity anoint her who is being baptized. But where there is a woman, and especially a deaconess, it is not fitting that women should be seen by men: but with the imposition of hand do thou anoint the head only. As of old the priests and kings were anointed in Israel, do thou in like manner, with the imposition of hand, anoint the head of those who receive baptism, whether of men or of women; and afterwards – whether thou thyself baptize, or thou command the deacons or presbyters to baptize – let a woman deacon, as we have already said, anoint the women. But let a man pronounce over them the invocation of the divine Names in the water. And when she who is being baptized has come up from the water, let the deaconess receive her, and teach and instruct her how the seal of baptism ought to be (kept) unbroken in purity and holiness. For this cause we say that the ministry of a woman deacon is especially needful and important. For our Lord and Saviour also was ministered unto by women ministers, Mary Magdalene, and Mary

the daughter of James and mother of Jose, and the mother of the sons of Zebedee [Mt 27:56], with other women beside. And thou also hast need of the ministry of a deaconess for many things; for a deaconess is required to go into the houses of the heathen where there are believing women, and to visit those who are sick, and to minister to them in that of which they have need, and to bathe those who have begun to recover from sickness.[28]

As this quote suggests, the central role of a deaconess was to anoint women with the holy oil, and upon the completion of the baptism, a priest or a bishop only anointed the baptised woman's forehead. Subsequently, the deaconess again assumed responsibility, now for the baptised woman's spiritual instruction. According to the Syriac *Didascalia*, since the bishop represents God and the priest represents Christ, the deaconess, in her role, symbolised the presence of the Holy Spirit and, for that reason, it was necessary to show her proper respect.[29]

Indeed, the practice of anointing with oil is as ancient in the East and the Jewish oikumene as the ceremony of baptising or washing with water. Without delving into theological and historical details, it should be mentioned that Christianity, which originated in the Jewish oikumene, has adopted and universalised the religious element of ordaining the Old Testament kings and, in some exceptional cases, the prophets, into its newly formed church, integrating it with the ceremony of baptism. In contrast to the Old Testament, the Christian baptism was not merely a washing-away of the sins with water, but, based on the testimony of the Forerunner, it was primarily baptism "with the Holy Spirit,"[30] which was expressed through the mystery of applying a blessed oil or the holy myrrh. Through the act of immersion in water and emerging from it, the individual, who is baptised in the mystery of Christ's death and resurrection, is "sealed" with the graces that spring from the Holy Spirit. This happens by means of anointing with the material oil or through the mystery of the seal. However, in the early church, they did not just seal the forehead and some parts of the body, the baptised individual's entire body was also

---

28   Hugh R. Connolly (trans.), *Didascalia Apostolorum: The Syriac Version Translated and Accompanied by the Verona Latin Fragments*, Oxford, 1929, pp. 146-148. Cf. Hans Achelis and Johannes Flemming (trans. and eds.), *Die Syrische Didaskalia*, Leipzig, 1904, 84-85.

29   See Josef Höfer and Karl Rahner (eds.), *Lexikon für Theologie und Kirche*, Vol. III, Freiburg, 1959, pp. 371-372; Tashean, *Vardapetut'iwn Aṛak'elots' anvawerakan kanonats' mateaně*; Vazgen Hakobyan (ed.), *Kanonagirk' Hayots'* (Book of Canon Law of Armenians), Vol. 1, Yerevan, 1964, pp. 18-66.

30   See Mt 3:11.

anointed. It was in this situation when the baptised person was a mature woman that the presence of deaconesses would become necessary. When immersing a newly converted woman in the water during the baptism ceremony, the bishop, or the priest, following Jesus' dominical order, would invoke only the Holy Trinity, "in the name of the Father and of the Son and of the Holy Spirit," [31] as a proclamation of its Christian essence, while the deaconess would generously anoint the woman's entire body with oil.

Apostolic Constitutions (4th c.)
(Διαταγαί των Αγίων Αποστόλων διά του Κλήμεντος)

The *Apostolic Constitutions* is an independent collection of eight closely connected books which were apparently edited at the end of the fourth century. It contains canons on Christian discipline, worship, and teaching, intended as an instruction manual for the clergy and, to some extent, also for the laity. Its creation was attributed to the Apostles, whose commandments were passed down by Clement of Rome (50-97, or 101 CE). The Church, however, has never entirely accepted its apostolic origin. Even the Council in Trullo, convened in 692, declared it invalid on the grounds that it had been adulterated by the heretics.

The *Apostolic Constitutions* assigned a central position to deaconesses because the rank of widows had begun to disappear gradually. A deaconess could be a widowed woman or a virgin who obeyed the ecclesiastical authority of a male deacon. While a deaconess symbolised the presence of the Holy Spirit and should accordingly be honoured; at the same time, "as we cannot believe in Christ without the teaching of the Spirit," the deaconess did not operate in the community without the deacon's instructions. [32] During the reception of the communion, she did not stand in the line of men but occupied the first position among widows and virgins. The deaconess became a clergy member, having been anointed by the bishop. Here, too, her role was to be useful during baptism, but she did not have the right to impart spiritual care or preaching. The deaconess could not give blessings in the Church or perform any ritual that formed part of the deacon's or priest's responsibilities. Outside the formal ritual responsibilities, the bishop might have assigned the

---

31   See Mt 28:19.
32   See Alexander Roberts and James Donaldson (eds.), *The Writings of the Fathers Down to AD 325*, Ante-Nicene Fathers, Vol. VII. Book II, xxv, Peabody, Massachusetts, 1995, p. 410.

deaconess a task to convey his message to other congregations and establish relations with the women and the higher ecclesiastical authorities of the congregation. Washing the bodies of deceased women was also considered one of the most important responsibilities of deaconesses.

So, we can see that even though the *Apostolic Constitutions* confers a special meaning to the anointment ceremony of deaconesses, it still strictly forbade them from undertaking preaching responsibilities and performing any service on the altar.

The Testament of Jesus Christ (5th c.)

The *Testament of Jesus Christ* is a Christian text which belongs to the genre of the ancient church orders. This work can be dated to the fifth century, although it could also have been edited in the fourth century. Like the previous texts, this, too, is believed to have originated in the Syriac-speaking milieu, though Egypt and Asia Minor could also have been its place of origin. The author is unknown, but the text conveys that it was a tradition passed down to His apostles by Jesus Christ before His ascension and indicates that the Lord has entrusted them with His words and commandments for the governance of the Church.[33]

The *Testament of Jesus Christ* was originally written in Greek; however, the complete text was first published in 1899 and translated into Latin from Syriac by the Syrian Catholic patriarch Ephrem Rahmani.[34]

The most remarkable aspect of this work is the exceptional role assigned to women. It has "widows who sit in front"[35] or priestesses, thirteen (or three)[36] in number, deaconesses, virgins, and widows, who received the donations made to the church. The widows, who were deemed the worthiest from among them, occupied an honourable and important position.[37] This was a

---

33   See James Cooper and Arthur J. Maclean (trans. and eds.), *The Testament of Our Lord*, Edinburgh, 1902, pp. 3, 49-50.

34   See Ephrem Rahmani, *Testamentum Domini nostri Jesu Christi nunc primum editur, latine reddidit et illustravit*, Mainz, 1899.

35   See Mayer, *Monumenta de viduis diaconissis virginibusque tractantia*, p. 29; Cooper and Maclean, *The Testament of Our Lord*, p. 99.

36   On the discrepancy in the numbers, see Cooper and Maclean, *The Testament of Our Lord*, pp. 191-192.

37   See Mayer, *Monumenta de viduis diaconissis virginibusque tractantia*, p. 29; Cooper and Maclean, *The Testament of Our Lord*, p. 99.

unique phenomenon which was unfortunately condemned by the Council of Laodicea in 364.

Widows were granted a prominent position in the Testament of Jesus Christ, and even deaconesses came under their authority. The title of "widow" was bestowed on women through blessing, though this should not be treated as a ritual anointing. However, there are parallels between the rank of widows and the institution of the diaconate: for example, their assigned permanent position on the bishop's left during a ceremony. Still, widows were deprived of the pastoral mission because their life was dedicated to hermitic ideals. This is the reason why deaconesses were involved in the pastoral mission and widows were not, even though they were under the authority of widows.

Archaeologists have unearthed a fourth- or fifth- century Byzantine basilica in the Israeli seaside city of Ashdod, which honours both the male and the female clergy. The inscriptions in the funerary mosaics also commemorate the names of deaconesses. The Greek inscription in the photo reads: "In memory of the priest Gaianos and Severa the deaconess." It dates back to 416 CE.

Icon of the deaconess Olympias of Constantinople (368-408 CE).

Deaconesses in the Byzantine Tradition

From the fourth century onwards, numerous prominent deaconesses were known within the Byzantine Church. This includes deaconess Olympias, who was a relative of John Chrysostom (344-407), Macrina, who was the sister of Basil of Caesarea (330-379) and Gregory of Nyssa (335/340-394). The latter's wife Theosebia was also a deaconess, and there were others. In this period, deaconesses were primarily the relatives of various religious figures, such as their mothers, sisters, or spouses. It was at the Council of Trullo (692) that a decision was made that once a priest ascended to the rank of bishop, his wife was expected to maintain a separate residence from him.

In the Byzantine Church, the tradition of the ordination of women deaconesses was practised until 10th–11th centuries, after which it gradually weakened.

An exciting testimony has been preserved from this time period, which is within the manuscript Barberini Gr. 336, also known as the Nicolai Manuscript or the Euchologion of Saint Mark.[38] The manuscript, copied in around 780 in southern Italy from a Constantinopolitan original, contains information about the practice, present in the Byzantine Church from the third to the eighth centuries, of ordaining deaconesses.

These canons, detailing the ordaining of deaconesses and preserved in Greek, were used by the Byzantine Greek bishops until the early Middle Ages. Nicholas Nicoli bought this manuscript in around 1400 and donated it to the Convent of San Marco in Florence in 1441. In around 1650, Carlo Strozzi presented the manuscript as a gift to Cardinal Francesco Barberini, and in 1902, it became part of the Vatican Library, where it is still kept to this day.

Its content is remarkable, for it bears a resemblance to the tradition of the ordination of deaconesses of the Armenian canon, which will be discussed in detail below. We should not disregard the possibility that both the Byzantine and Armenian canons had the so-called Q source from the early period of the church, which may be why they corresponded in content.

Here is the canon preserved in the manuscript Barberini Gr. 336:

---

38   All details regarding this manuscript, including the English translation of the text, have been taken from the website of the Wijngaards Institute for Catholic Research; see John Wijngaards (trans.), "The Barberini gr. 336 Manuscript", <https://www.womendeacons.org/rite-manuscript-barberini-gr-336/>, accessed on 23 September 2023.

§1. 'Prayer at the ordination (χειροτονία) of a deaconess'.

§2. After the sacred offertory[39], the doors [of the sanctuary – εἰκουοστάσιου] are opened and, before the Deacon starts the litany 'All Saints', the woman who is to be ordained Deacon is brought before the [Arch]bishop. And after he has said the 'Divine Grace' [statement] with a loud voice, the woman to be ordained bows her head. The Bishop imposes his hand on her forehead, makes the sign of the cross on it three times, and prays:

§3. "Holy and Omnipotent Lord, through the birth of your Only Son our God from a Virgin according to the flesh, you have sanctified the female sex. You grant not only to men, but also to women the grace and coming of the Holy Spirit. Please, Lord, look on this your maid servant and dedicate her to the task of your diaconate, and pour out into her the rich and abundant giving of your Holy Spirit.

Preserve her so that she may always perform her ministry (λειτουργεία) with orthodox faith and irreproachable conduct, according to what is pleasing to you.

For to you is due all glory and honour."

§4. After the 'Amen', one of the (other) Deacons now starts this prayer: 'Let us implore the Lord in peace.

For peace from above, let us pray the Lord.

For peace in the whole world.

For this our Archbishop, for his priestly ministry, his reward, his endurance, his peace and salvation and the work of his hands, let us pray to the Lord.

For (the name of the woman) who is to receive the diaconate and for her salvation. That God who loves people grant her a pure and immaculate diaconate, let us pray to the Lord.

For our pious Emperor who is protected by God, etc. etc.'

§5. While the Deacon makes these intercessions, the Archbishop, still imposing his hand on the head of the ordinand, prays as follows:

---

39 This is the part of the Holy Liturgy when the Sacred Elements – the bread and the wine – are brought in a solemn procession onto the altar.

§6. "Lord, Master, you do not reject women who dedicate themselves to you and who are willing, in a becoming way, to serve your Holy House, but admit them to the order of your ministers (λειτουργῶν).

Grant the gift of your Holy Spirit also to this your maid servant who wants to dedicate herself to you, and fulfil in her the grace of the ministry of the diaconate, as you have granted to Phoebe the grace of your diaconate, whom you had called to the work of the ministry (λειτουργία).

Give her, Lord, that she may persevere without guilt in your Holy Temple, that she may carefully guard her behaviour, especially her modesty and temperance.

Moreover, make your maid servant perfect, so that, when she will stand before the judgement seat of your Christ, she may obtain the worthy fruit of her excellent conduct, through the mercy and humanity of your Only Son."

§7. After the 'Amen', (the Archbishop) puts the stole of the diaconate (το διακονικόν οράριον) round her neck, under her (the woman's) scarf (μαφόριον), arranging the two lengths of the scarf towards the front.

§8. When (at the time of communion) the newly ordained woman has taken part of the sacred body and precious blood, the Archbishop hands her the chalice. She accepts it and puts it on the holy table (of the altar).

Deaconesses in the Syrian Church

As mentioned above, as an ecclesiastical function, the women's diaconate is a product of the Syriac-speaking milieu and ecclesiastical tradition. This tradition flourished both in the Syrian Jacobite and Nestorian Churches until the 11th century. In both churches, a deaconess had various responsibilities and functions. Here, we can observe that the deaconess not only received a special ordination, but during the liturgy, she also ascended to the altar, bringing onto it the Holy Bread and the Cup of Immortality and did the reading from the Gospel.

The ordination of deaconesses in the Greek-speaking and Syriac-speaking milieux of the early Christian communities largely had the form of a sacramental rite and was the same as the ordination of male deacons. In other words, it was not a mere blessing bestowed by a bishop or a simple priest but a sacrament. In this respect, the following particulars are worth mentioning:

i.   In the ordination rituals, for both deacons and deaconesses, the ordination is referred to as χειροτονία or χειροθεσία, derived from the Greek, meaning "to put the hands on" or "to anoint".

ii. Both the deacon and the deaconess are ordained by the bishop.

iii. The ordination of deacons and deaconesses occurs in front of the holy altar during the holy liturgy, while the conferral of the ranks of subdeacons and *dpir*s takes place amongst the clergy and not during the holy liturgy.

iv. The bishop ordains both of them by putting his hands on their heads through the authority of apostolic succession. To perform the ordination, he employs the element of the sacred mystery, which is none other than the ceremony of laying hands on the heads of the newly initiated individuals.

v.   The bishop offers a prayer for the bestowal of the Holy Spirit upon the deacon and deaconess by invoking the Spirit with the words 'receive the Holy Spirit ...'. In this way, the performance of the sacred mystery is enacted.

vi. Initially, individuals to be ordained as deacon, either a man or a woman, wait opposite the stairs that go on to the altar area. Then, accompanied by psalms and *sharakan*s (hymns), they are led onto the altar, where they are ordained with great solemnity as deacons by the bishop.

vii. The bishop performs the ordination with characteristic prayers, which testify to the sacred nature of the ceremony.

viii. For the deacon, as well as for the deaconess, the bishop discreetly pronounces the prayer 'The God's grace', which also is a sign of conferring a hierarchical rank of the church.

ix. The solemnity of the ceremony and the presence of a multitude of priests and attendees transform the ordination into a public event imbued with a festive ambience.

x. Both the deacon and the deaconess receive their orarion through ordination as an external symbol of their service and ecclesiastical rank, representing their voluntary acceptance of Christ's yoke.

xi. The newly initiated deacon and deaconess receive the holy chalice of communion in order to partake in the sacrament; the deaconess then takes it back and puts it on the altar.

The ordination of deaconesses indisputably carried an aspect of sacred mystery. The rituals of the ordination of men and women are notably similar in their content and form and reflect the intention of the ordaining bishop to bestow upon the initiated the rank of the ecclesiastical and spiritual service.[40]

Considering the preceding discussion, we conclude that in the history of the Church, the extended era spanning the 4th to the 11th centuries marked the classical period of the development of the women's diaconate, after which it gradually declined in prominence. The Armenian Church is the only exception to this.

---

40   Cf. Michael Mayr (trans.), "Die Weihe von Frauen zu Diakoninnen", *Wijngaards Institute for Catholic Research*, <https://womenpriests.org/de/tradition-de/deacord-die-weihe-von-frauen-%20zu-diakoninnen/>, accessed 15 January, 2024.

The Greek inscription in the mosaic, "Theodora the Bishop", is from the ninth century. It is located within the Church of Saint Praxedis the Martyr in Rome in the chapel of Bishop Zeno of Verona. The distinguished title belongs to Theodora, the mother of Pope Paschal I. The latter commissioned the construction of the chapel in her honour while she was still alive; the square halo in the mosaic demonstrates this latter fact.

Based on the mosaic inscription "THEODORA EPISCOPA", some scholars have concluded that Theodora was actually a bishop. They have noted that linguistically "episcopa" in Latin is the feminine form of the Greek "episcopos", which stands as evidence of the ordination of women within the Christian Church during the ninth century. It is evident that at some point in the past, the final letter "a" of the word "episcopa" was made illegible through scraping because the individuals who did it were well informed that the word "episcopa" indicated an ecclesiastical rank.

Catholic theologians have opposed this interpretation, noting that in the early Christian period, it was customary to call the wives and mothers of high-ranking clergy by the titles of their husbands or sons, as was the case with Theodora, for she is remembered as Pope Paschal I's mother.

Deaconesses in the Armenian Church

The first documentary source in the study of material from the Armenian Church is the *Kanonagirkʻ Hayotsʻ* (The Book of Canon Law of Armenians), which is a collection of medieval Armenian church law consisting of spiritual-ecclesiastical, ceremonial, confessional, ethical, and other canons that deal with communal issues assembled in separate groups of canons. The first collector and editor of the canons was the eighth-century Armenian, Catholicos Hovhannēs III Imastasēr Ōdznetsʻi, whose preliminary collection consisted of 24 groups of canons, 15 of which were translated from the Greek original, whereas the remaining nine groups consisted of canons of national ecclesiastical councils and the canons adopted by the Armenian Church Fathers. New groups of canons were added to the *Book of Canon Law of Armenians* in the mid-tenth century, and between the 11th and 17th centuries, the collection was again edited and completed with additional canons.[41]

While there are few mentions of deaconesses in the *Book of Canon Law of Armenians*, they still offer valuable insights into the subject at hand. Here, we should mention Canon XIX[42] of the Ecumenical Council of Nicaea convened in 325, which addresses the issue of the rebaptism of those followers of the heretical bishop Paul of Samosata who sought readmission into the church. It is of particular note because the deaconesses appointed by Paul rejected his heresy and returned to the Universal Church:

> Concerning the Paulicians who return to the catholic Church, a decree has been adopted according to which they must absolutely be rebaptized.[43] If

---

41 See Vazgen Hakobyan (ed.). *Kanonagirkʻ Hayotsʻ* (The Book of Canon Law of Armenians), Vol. I and II, Yerevan, 1964 and 1971.

42 Canon XIX relates to the issue of readmission of the adherents of the heresy of Paul of Samosata into the Universal Church. The followers of Paul lived in Syria from 200 to 276. This canon is of interest to us because it pertains to deaconesses. The deaconesses appointed by Paul rejected his heresy and returned to the Universal Church.

43 Paul of Samosata rejected the Holy Trinity because he professed Monarchianism, which claimed that there was only one unified God and treated Christ exclusively as a divine individual achieved through his baptism or simply as a phenomenon of God's manifestation. Athanasius of Alexandria argued that even though the followers of Paul of Samosata administered baptisms in the name of the Trinity, they did not do so in the orthodox manner, rendering their baptisms invalid and, consequently, it was necessary for them to be rebaptised when returning to the

some of them were before members of their clergy, they may, after being re-baptized, be ordained by the bishop of the catholic Church on condition, however, that they appear without stain and blameless.[44] But if an inquiry shows that they are unacceptable, they must appropriately be deposed. The same principle is to be observed for the deaconesses[45] and in general for all the members of the clergy.[46] We have mentioned the deaconesses serving in this condition although they have not received the imposition of hands, and they [i.e. the deaconesses who followed Paul of Samosata – A.M.] must absolutely be counted among the laity.[47]

In the commentary section of the *Book of Canon Law of Armenians*, Vazgen Hakobyan has added the following important observation, which is that the Nicene Canon XIX's "final section related to deaconesses is slightly abridged in comparison to the Greek version":

Ὡσαύτως δὲ καὶ περὶ τῶν διακονισσῶν, καὶ ὅλως περὶ τῶν ἐν τῷ κανόνι (Σύν, II, ἐν τῷ κλήρῳ) ἐξεταζομένων, ὁ αὐτὸς τύπος παραφυλαχθήσεται. Ἐμνήσθη μεν (Σύν, II, L., ἐμνήσθημεν) δὲ τῶν (L., without τῶν) διακονισσῶν τῶν ἐν τῷ σχήματι ἐξετασθεισῶν, ἐπεὶ μηδὲ χειροθεσίαν τινὰ ἔχουσιν, ὥστε ἐξά-παντος ἐν τοῖς λαϊκοῖς αὐτὰς ἐξετάζεσθαι.

Universal Church (see St Athanasius. *Selected Works and Letters*. Edited by Philip Schaff and Henry Wace, Peabody, Massachusetts, 1892, pp. 371-372).

44   Because the baptism of Paul of Samosata was invalid, the ordination was also deemed invalid. Hence, those who returned to the Catholic Church from this heresy were supposed to be rebaptised.

45   The Armenian version has "deacons".

46   The same treatment awaited the deaconesses who followed Paul of Samosata: if they were worthy of it, they would be rebaptised and ordained again by the bishop.

47   Peter L'Huillier, *The Church of the Ancient Councils: The Disciplinary Work of the First Four Ecumenical Councils*. Crestwood, NY, 1996, pp. 78-79. L'Huillier's translation is based on the Greek original, which, as we shall see below, is slightly different from the Armenian version. Որք հերձուածեցան ի հերձուածս Պաւ-ղոսիկեայի հերձուածողի եւ յետ այսորիկ ապաւինեցան ի կաթողիկէ եկե-ղեցի՝ սահման եղեալ է, զի դարձեալ մկրտեսցին ի կաթողիկէ եկեղեցի, զի այն ոչ լիութեամբ էր. ապա եթէ ոք ի նոցանէ յանցեալ ժամանակս ընդ ուխ-տին լինին, զի թէ ամիրօք կամ անարատք գտանիցին, ձեռնադրեսցին յե-պիսկոպոսէն եկեղեցւոյ սրբոյ. ապա եթէ ի հարցանելն եւ ի քննելն անա-րատք չգտանիցին, արժան է լքեցուցանել զայնպիսին: Սոյնպէս եւ վասն սարկաւագացն եւ ամենայն ոք որ եւ իցեն ընդ կանոնաւք, նոյն կարգ կացցէ: Յիշեցաք եւ վասն սարկաւագացն կանանց, որք կերպարանաւք ձեռնա-դրութիւն ունին, զի ամենայն իրաւք իբրեւ զմի յաշխարհականացն կացցեն:

As we can note, the Greek text speaks of deaconesses, while in Armenian, on one occasion, it is "for the deacons" and in the other instance, "the women deacons". In both cases, we should accept the reading "deaconesses".[48]

At this stage, it is worth turning to the decision regarding deaconesses adopted in 451 at the Council of Chalcedon:

> Canon XV: A woman must not be ordained deacon before the age of 40 and that after a careful inquiry. If after having received ordination and after having exercised her ministry for some time, she wants to marry, thereby scorning the grace of God, let her be excommunicated as well as him who has united himself to her.[49]

This canon is not included in the *Book of Canon Law of Armenians,* as the Armenian Church, owing to the military confrontation between Armenia and Sassanian Iran, did not participate in the Council of Chalcedon and subsequently altogether refused to accept its teachings and canonical decisions. Nonetheless, we need to examine the Universal Church and also search for initial signs in the overall history of the church. Here we encounter the law of Theodosius from 21 June 390, which set the age for the deaconesses at 60 years old.[50] In Canon XV of the Council of Chalcedon mentioned earlier, it was set at 40. As we saw above, if she married after the ordination, the deaconess would face the severe punishment of excommunication. Deaconesses were acknowledged as civil servants in the laws implemented by Emperor Justinian.[51] Amongst the 425 members of the clergy at the Hagia Sophia Church in Constantinople, it is known that there were 40 deaconesses, who either resided with their families or lived together in close proximity to the church. It

---

48 Hakobyan, *Kanonagirkʿ Hayotsʿ*, Vol. I, p. 565.

49 L'Huillier, *The Church of the Ancient Councils,* p. 243; "Can 15. Diaconissam non esse mulierem ordinandam ante annum quadragesimum, et eam cum accurata examinatione. Si auten postquam ordinatione sucepta ministerio aliquo tempore permansit seipsam matromonio tradiderit, dei gratiae iniuriam faciens, ea una com illo, qui ei coniunctus est, anathematizetur": MANSI VII, 363 (see John Wijngaards (trans.), "The Thirty Canons of the Holy and Fourth Council of Chalcedon", *Wijngaards Institute for Catholic Research,* <https://www.women-deacons.org/minwest-council-of-calcedon-451ad/>, accessed on 15 January 2024).

50 Clyde Pharr (ed. and trans.). *The Theodosian Code and Novels and the Sirmondian Constitutions.* Princeton, 1952, 16.2.27, p. 444.

51 *Iustiniani Novellae* 3, 1, (ed. Schoell-Kroll p. 20 sq.), in: Mayer, *Monumenta de viduis diaconissis virginibusque tractantia,* pp. 34-35.

appears that the existence of deaconesses and the development of their ecclesiastical role in the Western Church came to an end with the Council of Chalcedon.

Returning to the mentions of deaconesses in the *Book of Canon Law of
Armenians*, in Canon XVI of the group of canons attributed to the Armenian
Catholicos Saint Sahak, we find the following directives:

> Baptise with awe, and the women have no right to stand next to the priests,
> which some have turned into a habit of doing boldly and to baptise with them
> [i.e. the priests]; instead, they should pray in their places.[52]

The same canon is reaffirmed in Canon XVI of the second Council of Dvin in
554/555:

> And women have no right to stand next to the priests, for it should be the
> deacons who will serve them. And women ought to pray in their places and
> should not assist the priests, for we have heard that they replace the dea-
> cons.[53]

In both cases, it is evident that the women mentioned in these canons were
likely deaconesses who chose not to confine themselves to their designated
responsibilities during the baptism ceremony, but instead, they endeavoured
to participate in the sacred mystery alongside the priests. According to the
canons attributed to Catholicos Sahak and the canons of the second Council
of Dvin, this phenomenon was considered erroneous.[54]

---

52   Hakobyan, *Kanonagirkʿ Hayotsʿ*, vol. I, pp. 377–378: Մկրտութիւն առնել երկիւ-
ղածութեամբ, եւ կանայք ի ժամ մկրտութեանն մերձ առ քահանային մի՛
իշխեցեն կալ, որպէս սովորեցին ումանք առնել յանդգնաբար եւ մկրտել ընդ
նոսա, այլ ի տեղւոյ իւրեանց աղաւթեցեն: See Melikʿ-Tʿangean, *Hayotsʿ
ekeghetsʿakan irawunkʿĕ*, Vol. I, p. 536.

53   Hakobyan, *Kanonagirkʿ Hayotsʿ*, vol. I, p. 485: Եւ կանայք առ քահանայս մի՛
իշխեցեն կալ, բայց սարկաւագունքն սպասաւորեցեն, եւ կանայք իւր-
եանց տեղին աղաւթեցեն, եւ մի՛ եղիցին գործակիցք քահանայիցն, որպէս
լսեմք, ունելով զտեղիս սարկաւագացն: This canon appears under the title
"Kanonkʿ Nersēsi Katʿoghikosi ew Nershaphoy Mamikonēitsʿ Episkoposi:
Glukh[kʿ] 37" (Canons of the Armenian Catholicos Nersēs and Bishop Nersha-
puh Mamikonean: XXXVII Chapters) in the *Book of Canon Law of Armenians*.
See also Melikʿ-Tʿangean, *Hayotsʿ ekeghetsʿakan irawunkʿĕ*, Vol. I, p. 380, and
Abēl Mkhitʿareantsʿ, *Patmutʿiwn Zhoghovotsʿ Hayastaneaytsʿ Ekeghetsʿwoy* (His-
tory of the Councils of the Armenian Church), Vagharshapat, 1874, p. 80.

54   See Melikʿ-Tʿangean, *Hayotsʿ ekeghetsʿakan irawunkʿĕ*, Vol. I, p. 536.

Contrary to what we observed earlier – that the *Book of Canon Law of Armenians* and other documents of our church lack extensive information about deaconesses – this tradition is not entirely unfamiliar to the Armenian Church Fathers. The *Haykazean Baṛgirkʿ*, which relies on the vocabulary of the Golden Age translations of our Fathers, defines the word "deaconess" as "a woman official or a virgin serving the church, as well as a Mother of a nunnery".[55] Stepʿan Malkhaseantsʿ, in turn, explains the word in the following way: "A virgin who serves as a deacon in the church. According to the ecclesiastical laws, women can be ordained as deaconesses but never as priests".[56]

It is interesting that while in the Middle Ages in the Western Catholic and Eastern Orthodox Churches, women were gradually pushed away from holding hierarchical positions in the church, the garden of the Armenian church grafted its vine-plant by upholding the religious tradition of deaconesses. We can read about this in the following testimony in the *Mashtotsʿ* ritual book edited in the ninth-tenth centuries:

> Women, on the other hand, should be given a habit, and the same rite should be performed. However, let the deaconesses take off their [worldly clothes], covering their forehead with a black veil to the eyebrows.[57]

In this example, the word *sarkawag* (deacon) contains the characteristic feminine suffix *-uhi*, that is, *sarkawaguhi* (deaconess). It is evident that this refers to virgins who made vows for monastic life, and that they were to be dressed by a deaconess. This message is found at the conclusion of the section that describes a rite entitled "Ordination of those who will be worthy of monastic life", and it naturally leads one to believe that in medieval Armenia, women who took monastic vows, received consecration or, at the very least, a blessing through consecration.

---

55 See Awetikʿean, Gabriel, Siwrmelean, Khachʿatur, and Mkrtichʿ Awgerean (eds.), *Nor Baṛgirkʿ Haykazean Lezui* (New Dictionary of the Armenian Language), Vol. II, Yerevan, 1981, p. 701.

56 Stepʿan Malkhaseantsʿ (ed.), *Hayerēn Batsʿatrakan Baṛaran* (Dictionary of Armenian Language), Vol. IV, Yerevan, 1944, p. 193.

57 *Mayr Mashtotsʿ* (Ritual Book), Gēorg Tēr-Vardanean (ed.), Vol. I, Book I, Surb Ejmiatsin, 2012, p. 329: Իսկ կանաց պարտ է սքեմ տալ եւ զնոյն կատարել կարգս։ Բայց հոլանի սարկաւագուհիքն արասցեն, սեւ փակեղամբ ծածկե[ս]ցեն զճակատն մինչեւ յաւնսն. See also MS 457 of the Mekhitarist Library of Venice in *Mayr tsʿutsʿak hayerēn dzeṛagratsʿi Venetik* (Catalogue of Armenian Manuscripts of Venice), Barsegh Sargisean and Grigor Sargisean (eds.), Vol. III, Venice, 1966, pp. 27-33, in particular p. 32, folio 126v.

Evidence from the Eighth Century:
The First Armenian Female Hymnographers

The mellifluous lyre of the *sharakan*s of the Armenian Church has also been sounded by women who were inspired by the Holy Spirit. Among them, Sahakdukht Siwnets'i and Khosrovidukht Goght'nats'i undoubtedly stand out.[58] Even though our manuscript sources do not attest to their religious dedication, such as being part of the diaconate or holding any other title, their life and work, especially those of Sahakdukht Siwnets'i, allow us to assume that they had acquired a certain status in the church. In other words, they held an office of which the authority and position, unfortunately, remain unknown to us. Nonetheless, it is worth making a brief reference to women such as hermit Sahakdukht Siwnets'i and noblewoman Khosrovidukht Goght'nats'i, who both gifted the sweet-scented flowers of their heart and soul to the Armenian literary tradition, and by their impressive example indicate the significant role that women played in the earliest stages of the development of our church, including writing music, hymns, melodies, and canticles.

---

58 For more details, see Garegin Yovsep'eants', *Mkhit'ar Ayrivanets'i: Noragyut ardzanagrut'iwn ew erker* (Mkhit'ar Ayrivanets'i: Newly Discovered Inscription and Works), Jerusalem, 1931, pp. 17-23; Step'anos Ōrbēlean, *Patmut'iwn Nahangin Sisakan* (History of the Sisakan Province), Vol. I, Paris, 1859, p. 182; Ghewond Alishan, *Sisakan: Teghagrut'iwn Siwneats'ashkharhi* (Sisakan: The Topography of the Land of Siwnik'), Venice, 1893, pp. 127-128; G.A. Hakobyan, "8-rd dari mer kin sharakanagirnerě" (Our Eighth-Century Women Authors of *Sharakan*s), *Ejmiatsin* 34 (3), 1977, pp. 20-25; Anna Arevshatyan, "Step'anos Siwnets'u vark'ě orpes vaghk'ristoneakan Hayastani erazhshtakan arvesti arzhek'avor patmakan aghbyur" (The Vita of Step'anos Siwnets'i as a Valuable Source of Early Christian Armenia's Musical Art), *Banber Matenadarani* 30, 2020, pp. 355-358; Ērna Shirinyan, "Aṛajin kin sharakanagirnerě" (The Fist Women Authors of *Sharakan*s), in: Festschrift in Honour of Armenuhi Drost-Abgarjan, forthcoming, Internationale Werkstücke – Deutsch Armenische Studien, University of Halle; Manea-Ērna S. Shirinian, "Saakdukht Siunetsi", *Pravoslavnaia Ėntsikopediia*, Vol. LX, Moscow, 2020, p. 739; Anna Arevshatyan, "Khosrovidukht", *K'ristonya Hayastan Hanragitaran*, Yerevan, 2002, p. 436; Mher Navoyan, "Sahakdukht", ibid., pp. 878-879; Y. K'ēōsēean, "Sahakdukht Siwnets'i", *Matenagirk' Hayots'*, VI, 8th Century, Antelias, Lebanon, 2007, pp. 601-605.

Sahakdukht Siwnets'i was the sister of the prominent seven-eighth-century historian Step'anos Siwnets'i, and she was commemorated in his vita in the following way:

> Saint Step'anos had a sister called Sahakdukht who had adopted a hermit's lifestyle, rejecting all the world's distractions. Leaving the city of Dvin, she settled in the deep valley of Garni near the Azat River [...] The location pleased her, and she settled in the abode of patriarch Saint Sahak, and it was in this same place that she died. She was adorned with all virtues and wisdom. She instructed innocent children, so that when they were of the right age, they would be ready to be ordained into the rank of priesthood. And she would sit behind a curtain and teach her students. She composed numerous canticles and melodies, Christmas carols and Assumption *kts'urd*s (hymns, anthems), one of which is "Holy Mary".[59]

According to Mkhit'ar Ayrivanets'i, Step'anos Ōrbēlean also wrote about Sahakdukht:

> She had a remarkable gift for musical art, and sitting behind a curtain, she would teach numerous people. And she composed *kts'urd*s and sweet-sounding melodies, one of which was "Holy Mary", which was composed in her name.[60]

---

59 Yovsep'eants', *Mkhit'ar Ayrivanets'i: Noragyut ardzanagrut'iwn ew erker*, pp. 18-19: Կայր քոյր մի սրբոյն Ստեփանոսի Սահակդուխտ անուն՝ ստացեալ վարս կուսականս եւ հրաժարեալ յամենայն սքանսանաց աշխարհիս. եղեալ ի քաղաքէն Դվնայ՝ բնակեցաւ ի խորային ձորին Գառնոյ առ Ազատ զետով [...] Անդ հաճեալ սուրբ կոյսն՝ բնակեցաւ ի կայարանի սրբոյն Սահակայ հայրապետին, եւ ի նմին վախճանեցաւ: Սա էր զարդարեալ ամենայն առաքինութեամբ եւ իմաստութեամբ սնուցանէր մանկունս անարատս, եւ աճեալ ի չափի հասակի, կարգէր ի քահանայութեան. իսկ ինքն ի ներքոյ վարագուրի նստելով, ուսուցանէր զաշակերտեալսն: Սա արար տաղս բազումս եւ մեղեդիս եւ կցուրդս ծննդեան եւ փոխմանն, յորոց մի է Սրբուհի Մարիամն:

60 Step'anos Ōrbēlean, *Patmut'iwn Nahangin Sisakan*, p. 182: Սա յոյժ հմուտ էր երաժշտական արիեստին, որ եւ ի ներքոյ վարագուրի նստեալ ուսուցանէր զբագումս: Եւ արար կցուրդս եւ մեղեդիս քաղցրեղանակս, յորոց մին՝ սրբուհի Մարիամ, որ իւրով անուամբ է յորինեալ:

Sahakdukht also authored a *kts'urd* in five stanzas dedicated to the Assumption of the Mother of God, beginning with the following lines: "Today, multitudes of apostles and virgins have gathered together".[61] Besides this, she composed the "Holy Mary, the Golden Trumpet", a modulated chant in the eighth tone, *grave*, of which only the first and the seventh stanzas have been preserved in the *Book of Hours* of the Armenian church.[62]

Despite the scarcity of historical sources, hermit Sahakdukht deserves open admiration both for her luminous individuality and for her oeuvre, which has resulted in fascination with Armenian virgins, thousands of women martyrs, and the sisters of charity. It is of utmost interest to note that in the eighth century, women had the choice to become hermits and devote themselves to an ascetic life in Ayrivank' and its vicinity, during a time when there were around 140 cave-cells inhabited by male hermits.[63]

One aspect of Christian beliefs, to live a life of continence, remains present in the traditions of sister churches to this day. For instance, on Mount Athos in Greece, a monastic peninsular where hundreds of people have dedicated themselves to an ascetic life, individuals live not only in monasteries but also in the caves of the mountains and valleys. However, women are strictly prohibited from entering or being present in this monastic republic, as it is inhabited exclusively by male coenobites. Conversely, there has been an unmistakable open-mindedness regarding the matter of gender within the Armenian Apostolic Church, as demonstrated by Sahakdukht's example. She led a life of continence in the sacred shadow of Ayrivank', in the "neighbourhood" or "vicinity" of male coenobites and hermits.

Indeed, within this context, the fact that Sahakdukht had the right to teach, albeit "behind a curtain", is even more remarkable, as "[s]he instructed innocent children, and bringing them to the right age, she would set them up in the rank of priesthood".[64] This means that she taught many clergy and helped them advance to the point where they were ordained as priests. The reference "she would set them up in the rank of priesthood" is the most significant privilege held by this eighth-century hermit, especially because dur-

---

61   See Arevshatyan, "Step'anos Siwnets'u vark'ĕ orpes vaghk'ristoneakan Hayastani erazhshtakan arvesti arzhek'avor patmakan aghbyur", pp. 355-356: Այսօր բազմութիւնք առաքելոց եւ կուսանաց ժողովեալ ի միասին:

62   Ibid., p. 356.

63   Shirinyan, "Aṛajin kin sharakanagirnerĕ" (forthcoming).

64   Yovsep'eants', *Mkhit'ar Ayrivanets'i: Noragyut ardzanagrut'iwn ew erker*, pp. 18-19.

ing this period, the role and presence of women in the church within the clerical order of sister churches were gradually being disregarded. This is a unique phenomenon within the Armenian Church and portrays the spiritual and ecclesiastical life of the early Middle Ages in new hues.

Examining the hermit's teaching "behind the curtain" is of equal significance. Sahakdukht may have been an attractive person who had dedicated herself to a life of abstinence. She deprived herself of all sensibilities that could have become a source of pleasure, in other words, of everything that could be pleasurable to the body. She went to great lengths to avoid tempting the young men who would come to her for instruction with her beauty, for the core principle of a life of continence is the rejection of worldly pleasures to avoid unintentional sin. Instead, one must unify with the spiritual realm with the aim of salvation through Christ. In Christian perception, sin is not solely an act that has already occurred but, above all, the temptation that arises within the thoughts and senses of an individual, leading them toward sin. Being "behind a curtain", Sahakdukht undoubtedly succeeded in hiding what may have been an attractive appearance from strangers' eyes, but her gentle voice? Well, it is impossible to teach music without singing. Can we not at all imagine her angelic, "sweet-sounding", and soul-stirring voice singing the sharakan "Holy Mary, the Golden Trumpet", dedicated to the Mother of God? That sound would undoubtedly awaken a pure emotion in virtuous hearts, evoking tears of repentance from our tearful eyes.

It would be erroneous to assume that her practice of teaching "behind a curtain" was connected to restrictions stemming from her being a woman. Instead, it was a result of her dedication to a life of abstinence. And regardless, she was a teacher though it may sound audacious, this means that in the eighth century, a woman claimed the authority to instruct, or, in other words, "to act as a vardapet (doctor of the church)." This was seven centuries before St Grigor Tat'ewats'i.

It was with Tat'ewats'i that the definitive authority to teach the orthodox faith and sacred traditions of the Armenian Church, through the bestowal of a corresponding teaching rank and sceptre, were established.

In the eighth century, Armenia was already entirely under Arab rule. At this time another radiant star, whose brilliance illuminated the spiritual poetry and musical art of Armenia, emerged in the Armenian skies. It was Lady Khosrovidukht, the sister of the prince of Goght'n Vahan Goght'nets'i. She composed a eulogy on her brother's martyrdom in the name of Christ, which starts with the lines, "The sound of lamentation is more astonishing to me than the melody of music".[65] Unlike Sahakdukht's sublime creations, the Armenian Church has canonised the eulogy above, introducing it as a *sharakan* in its *Hymnary*. To this day, it is the only musical piece sung in the canon about the day commemorating Vahan Goght'nets'i.[66] Understandably, to counterbalance the oppression of the Arab rule and encroachments of Islam, the Armenian Church showed a preference for this eulogy, as it expressed sentiments against Islam while honouring the Armenian saint who was martyred and shed his blood for the truth of Christ's faith.

In fact, within a global Christian context, these Armenian authors of *sharakans*, Sahakdukht the hermit and Lady Khosrovidukht, were the first female hymnographers in the Universal Church. They lived around a century prior to the Greek hymnographer Kassia of Constantinople (*ca* 810-855). Kassia gained prominence in the Byzantine Church for composing almost fifty hymns and spiritual verses, as well as 261 secular texts in the form of epigrams.[67]

65 Arevshatyan, "Step'anos Siwnets'u vark'ě orpes vaghk'ristoneakan Hayastani erazhshtakan arvesti arzhek'avor patmakan aghbyur", pp. 357-358; Shirinyan, "Aṛajin kin sharakanagirnerě" (forthcoming).

66 Arevshatyan, "Step'anos Siwnets'u vark'ě orpes vaghk'ristoneakan Hayastani erazhshtakan arvesti arzhek'avor patmakan aghbyur", p. 357.

67 See Diane Touliatos. "Kassia", *Grove Music Online*, 2001, <https://www.oxford-musiconline.com/grovemusic/view/10.1093/gmo/9781561592630.001.0001/omo-9781561592630-e-0000040895>; Joachim Schäfer, "Kassia die Hymnographin", *Ökumenisches Heiligenlexikon*, <https://www.heiligenlexikon.de/BiographienK/Kassia_Hymnographin.html>, accessed 15 January, 2024.

Evidence on Deaconesses from the 12th Century Onwards

Armenian historians provide actual evidence of deaconesses from the 12th century onwards. However, Patriarch Nersēs Shnorhali's "General Epistle", which was addressed to all segments of Armenian society, is particularly interesting, for the author made no mention of virgins and deaconesses. Does this mean that, in general, there were no female monasteries or women holding the office of deaconesses in Cilicia during the time of Shnorhali? Nersēs Lambronats'i, the famous bishop of fortified Lambron, who was a contemporary of Shnorhali, mentioned the following in his work "Deliberations on the Church Orders and an Exegesis of the Mystery of the Liturgy":

> And monastic life is considered of lesser rank, not only compared to the priesthood but also to the diaconate. For this is allowed to women, too, as Saint Basil writes, whereas the diaconate is certainly not.[68]

Nersēs Lambronats'i endorsed the tradition of women leading a monastic life, but he did not support the idea of them becoming deacons. Regardless, the tradition of bestowing the office of deacon upon women clearly existed in Cilicia as well. The prayer of blessing for the ordination of deaconesses would not have been included in the *Mashtots'* copied in Skevra in 1314, under the sponsorship and supervision of the Abbot of the Skevra Monastery Bishop Kostandin Pehests'i (or Pehesnats'i), if this concept had never been part of his thought and perception. Here is the original prayer included in the manuscript:

> Canon for the ordination of women deacons, who are deaconesses.
>
> Psalm 44[69]: "My heart overflows with a goodly theme ..." is said.
>
> Litany: "Let us implore in faith."
>
> And the following prayer is said: "Oh, Lord, benevolent and most merciful, all things were created by the words of Your command, and through the Incarnation of your Only Begotten Son, You have made men and women equal,

---

68 Nersēs Lambronats'i, *Khorhrdatsut'iwnk' i kargs ekeghets'woy ew meknut'iwn khorhrdoy pataragin* (Deliberations on the Church Orders and an Exegesis of the Mystery of the Liturgy), Venice, 1847, p. 53: և փորք է կրոնաւորութիւն ոչ միայն քան զքահանայութիւն, այլ և քան զսարկաւագութիւն. զի սա և կանանց է համարձակելի, որպէս և սուրբ Բարսեղ գրէ. իսկ սարկաւագութիւն և ոչ բնաւ:

69 This corresponds to Psalm 45 of the English Bible.

for it pleased You to bestow spiritual grace not only upon men but also upon women. Likewise, at this moment, choose your female servant to serve in Your holy church and grant her grace through the Holy Spirit so that she may remain blameless and pure in her righteous deeds through the mercy of Christ, with whom glory, dominion, and honour be to You, the Father of All, and to the lifegiving and redeeming Holy Spirit, now and for ever and unto ages of ages. Amen.[70]

In Chapter 225, titled "Concerning the statutes for the orders of the church and of the court of the king" of his *Datastanagirkʿ* (Book of Judgement), written in 1184, Mkhitʿar Gosh, a prominent author of the 12th century, wrote the following about deaconesses:

There are also deacons ordained from among the women, who are called "deaconesses," for the sake of preaching and reading the Gospel to the women, lest a man enter there or she go outside the convent. But when the priests perform baptism, they come to the font, because they wash the woman with the water of propitiation under the veil. Their habit is that common to all believers, save a cross is worn on the forehead, and they have a stole hanging down on the right side. Do not regard this as something new and irregular, because we have learned it from the tradition of the holy Apostle, since he says: "I entrust to you our sister Phoebe, who is a servant of the church."[71]

---

70   MS Matenadaran 2787, scribe – Nersēs, recipient – Bishop Kostandin Pehesntsʿi, folios 168r-168v:

Կանոն ձեռնադրութեան սարկաւագ կանանց, որ են սարկաւագուհիք:

Ասի Սաղմոս. ԽԴ. Բղխեացէ սիրտ իմ զպատգամս քո բարիս:

Քարոզէ. Խնդրեսցուք հաւատով:

Եւ ասէ զաղաւթս այս. Տէր բարերար եւ բազմագոյթ, որ զամենայն արարեր բանիւ հրամանի քո, եւ ի ձեռն մարմնաւոր տնտեսութեան Միածնիդ քում հաւասարեցուցեր զարուն եւ զէգն որպէս հաճոյ թուեցաւ քեզ ոչ միայն արանց այլ եւ կանանց տալ շնորհս հոգեւորս: Նոյնպէս եւ այժմ ընտրեա զաղախին քո առ ի պաշտաւն պիտոյից եկեղեցւոյ քո սրբոյ եւ տուր սմա շնորհս ի Հոգւոյդ Սրբոյ, զի պահեսցէ զսա անբիծ եւ անարատ ի գործս արդարութեան ողորմութեամբ Քրիստոսի քո: Ընդ որում քեզ Հաւր ամենակալի կենդանարար եւ ազատիչ Սուրբ Հոգւոյդ վայել է փառք, իշխանութիւն եւ պատիւ այժմ եւ միշտ եւ յաւիտեանս յաւիտենից. Ամէն: There is also another colophon of this manuscript that provides interesting details about Bishop Kostandin Pehesntsʿi (see folios 341r-341v).

71   Thomson, *Datastanagirkʿ of Mxitʿar Goš*, p. 278; Mkhitʿar Gosh, *Girkʿ Datastani*, pp. 136-137: Են եւ ի կանանց սարկաւագունք, որք կոչին սարկաւագուհիք, ձեռնադրեալս վասն քարոզելոյ կանանց եւ ընթեռնուլ Աւետարան, զի մի՞ մտցէ անդ այր, եւ մի՞ նա արտաքս, քան զկանսն, ելանիցէ: Բայց յորժամ

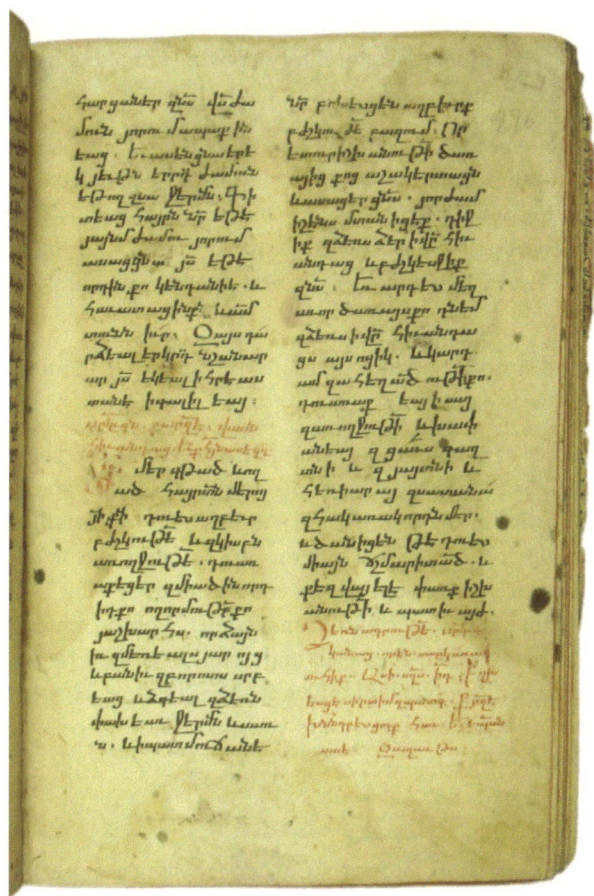

Canon "Ordination of women deacons who are deaconesses", MS Matenadaran 998, f. 226r, Mashtots' (Ritual Book); scribes – Yohanēs, Step'anos; recipient – vardapet Yohanēs; year – 1546.

մկրտութիւն առնեն քահանայքն, զան յալազանն, զի զկանայսն նոքա լուա-
նան չրով քաւութեանն՝ ներքոյ վարագուրին։ Սքեմ է նոցա ամենայն ինչ
հալատաւորաց, բայց ի ճակատն խաչ լինի, եւ քուրկեն ի յաշմէ կողմանէ ի
կախ ունելով։ Մի՛ ինչ նոր եւ անկարգ վարըցիս զայս, քանզի ի սրբոյ առաքելոյն աւանդութենէ ուսանիմք, քանզի ասէ՝ յանձն առնեմ ձեզ զՓիբէ քոյր
մեր, որ է սպասաւոր եկեղեցլոյն։ See also Vardan Hats'uni, *Hayuhin Patmu-
t'ean Arjew* (The Armenian Woman Facing History), Venice, 1936, pp. 152-153.

Chapter 229 of the *Datastanagirk'*, titled, "Concerning the statutes for those banished", explained the canon for deposing someone from the ecclesiastical rank of a deacon:

> Now if anyone becomes worthy of banishment among those who were ever of ecclesiastical rank, according to the law let it be handled as follows. Deacons and priests will be deposed by the bishops, because it is he who ordained them. Deaconesses by deacons; and laity and nuns and the religious, and those who ever were ordained by a priest, [will be excommunicated] by the priest.[72]

We can also find similar evidence pertaining deaconesses in Smbat Sparapet's *Datastanagirk'*, written in 1265:

> And [deacons] can read the Gospel and deliver sermons and bring the chalice from the sacristy onto the altar and sound the ripidion and burn incense, bring the chalice of the communion. And if the priest commands, they can also ordain deaconesses so that they too give sermons to women and read the Gospel in a place where men cannot enter. And their habit is that of the believers, and they can wash children and women with the water of atonement and bear a cross on their foreheads and a stole over their right shoulder. Armenian women abandoned this office at an earlier time. However, it refers to what the Apostle wrote: "I entrust to you our sister Phoebe, who is a servant of the church".[73]

---

72 Thomson, *Datastanagirk' of Mxit'ar Goš*, p. 285; Mkhit'ar Gosh, *Girk' Datastani*, p. 141: Արդ, եթէ արժանաւոր ոք աքսորանաց իցէ, որք միանգամ յեկեղեցական կարգէ իցեն, ըստ իրաւանց այպէս լիցի. սարկաւագք եւ քահանայք լուծցին յեպիսկոպոսաց, զի նա է ձեռնադրող նոցա. սարկաւագունիք` ի սարկաւագաց. եւ աշխարհականք, եւ հաւատաւորք, եւ կրաւնաւորք եւ որք միանգամ ի քահանայէ ձեռնադրին` ի քահանայէն: See also Heghine Mkrtchyan's interesting article "Sarkavaguhineri tsaṛayut'yunn u pashtonĕ Hay aṛak'elakan ekeghets'um" (The Service and the Office of Deaconesses in the Armenian Apostolic Church), *Ējmiatsin* 10, 2013, pp. 39-51; p. 42.

73 Smbat Sparapet, *Datastanagirk' Smbat ishkhani (Gundstabli)* (Book of Judgement of Prince Smbat (the Constable), edited by Arsēn Ghltchyan, Ejmiatsin, 1918, p. 40: Եւ կարեն աւետարան կարդալ ու քարոզ ասել եւ զսկիհն բերել ի սենեկէն ի սեղանն, եւ բշոց բշել, ու խունկ ծխել, եւ զհաղորդութեան սկիհն բերել. եւ թէ հրամայէ քահանայն, նա սարկաւագունիք էլ կարեն ձեռնադրել, որ եւ նոքա եւս կարեն քարոզ ասել կանանց, եւ աւետարան կարդալ, ուր եւ այր մարդ չմտնէ: Եւ սբեմ է նոցա հաւատաւորացն, եւ կարեն լուանալ տղայք եւ կանայք քաւութեան ջրովն, եւ խաչ ունենան ի ճակատն եւ բուշ կենայ ի յաջ թեւն. եւ ի Հայոց կանանց վաղ է ջնջած այս կարցս: Բայց այս այն է, զոր

It is worth noting that Smbat Sparapet attributed a much broader sphere of activity to deaconesses in the church. In fact, their mission was not limited to nunneries as they could also "wash children and women with the water of atonement". This leads us to assume that they held a similar office in the pastoral environment of the church.

We should nevertheless note that Smbat Sparapet's *Datastanagirk'* attributed the right to ordain deaconesses to deacons when he said, "If the priest commands, they [i.e. the deacons] can also ordain deaconesses". The same hierarchy can be observed in the canon of Mkhit'ar Gosh mentioned above, which discussed the deposition of deaconesses from their office: "Deacons and priests will be deposed by the bishops, because he it is who ordained them. Deaconesses by deacons..."[74] Apparently, both authors used the same source or drew upon an existing church tradition, the exploration of which is beyond the scope of this work.

Approximately a century later, the Archbishop of Siwnik' Step'anos Ōrbēlean, who can be considered the staunchest supporter of preserving the traditions of the Armenian Church, offered the following information about deaconesses in his *Patmut'iwn Nahangin Sisakan* (History of the Sisakan Province), composed in 1299:

> And among women, there are deaconesses who preach in the female monasteries. Their clothing is that of the believers: wearing a mantle and having a cross on the forehead and a small cape which goes under the right arm hanging from the robe or the belt, they ascend to the altar and preach and read the Gospel; yet, [they do the latter] not among the people on the altar but in a separate area or some corner. However, they may not participate in the service of the holy sacrament as the male deacons do.[75]

գրել է առաքեալն՝ թէ յանձն առնեմ ձեզ զՓիբէ՝ քոյր մեր, որ է սպասաւոր եկեղեցւոյն: See also A.G. Galstyan, *Datastanagirk'* (Book of Judgement), Yerevan, 1958, pp. 66-67 and Hats'uni, *Hayuhin Patmut'ean Aṛjew*, p. 153.

74 Thomson, *Datastanagirk' of Mxit'ar Goš*, p. 285.

75 Step'anos Ōrbēlean, *Patmut'iwn Nahangin Sisakan*, p. 153: Իսկ ի կանանց սարկաւագունիք լինին զի ի կանանց վանս քարոզեն. զգեստ է նոցա հաւատաւորացն, փիլոն արկանել եւ ի ճակատն խաչ ունել եւ փոքրիկ ուրարն յաջմէ ի ներքոյ բազկին զհանդերձէն կամ զգօտւոյն ի կախ ունելով ելանէ ի բեմն եւ քարոզէ եւ ընթեռնու աւետարան ոչ յամբոխին ի վերայ բեմին. այլ առանձինեն կամ յանկեան ուրեք. բայց ի սուրբ խորհրդոյն սպասաւորութիւն բնաւ մի հպեսցի որպէս արու սարկաւագունս: See also Hats'uni, *Hayuhin Patmut'ean Aṛjew*, p. 153.

Even though Step'anos Ōrbēlean, the Archbishop of Siwnik', did not consider it appropriate for the deaconess to read the Gospel or preach to people from the altar of the church, he affirmed the tradition that granted the title of deaconess to women. However, he restricted their responsibilities to women's monasteries, allowing them to preach and read the Gospel privately and discriminating against them by favouring male deacons during the service of the Holy Liturgy.

In the 11th–15th centuries, not all our clergy showed open-mindedness towards women holding office in the church. The unfriendly discourse on women by Pōghos Tarōnats'i, Grigor Tat'ewats'i, Yovhannēs Erznkats'i Pluz, Movsēs Erznkats'i, and many other doctors of the church was a result of serious confrontations when foreign groups, including directly the Greek Orthodox and Latin Churches, endeavoured to impose their teachings and ways of thinking on the beliefs, teaching principles, and traditions of Armenian Church through their representatives.

For instance, in one of his epistles, titled "Against the Roman Philosopher Theopistos", written within the context of the debates with the representatives of Syrian and Greek Churches over deaconesses and other traditions, *vardapet* Pōghos Tarōnats'i noted the following: "The Syrians order women to ascend to the altar, which is not right." He then added:

> They also allow women to ascend to God's Holy Altar, something foreign to Apostolic and Prophetic canons. Furthermore, the Holy Spirit also abhorred that women should step on the altar.

> And now, the law states that only Moses had the right to ascend to the summit of the mountain and speak to God, and the God-receiving altar of God follows this example. Meanwhile, all the priests stood in the middle of the mountain which represents this Church of Christ. And people stood at the foot of the mountain, which is the church's external chamber.

> That mountain was the prototype of this holy church, and this commandment was laid down under the old law that one should approach the holy mountain in holiness. And in the new law, this is what the scripture says, "Only James, brother of the Lord, had the right to enter the holy of holies." In the old [law], the mountain was ablaze with fire, while in the new one, it is this church, which is God's dwelling and the place of sacrifice of Christ's immolation of His blood.

> And this is the truth of Christ's economy, which the holy patriarchs, when gathered at Nicaea, affirmed by establishing anathemas and stating that it is not permissible for women to ascend to the bema.

Moreover, the Apostle Paul restricted the ranks of women and did not permit them to speak at all in church. And behold, they [i.e., the Syrians] went against Paul and permitted women on the bema.[76]

It is widely known that St Grigor Tat'ewats'i was one of the most eminent representatives from Eastern Christian doctors of the church leading the opposition against the Latin Church. In addition to opposing the Latin tradition regarding baptism, he also rejected its administration by women, even under extreme circumstances. In his valuable *Girk' Harts'mants'* (Book of Questions), he wrote:

> Again, it is known that the heretical nation of the Franks states that though baptism is the priest's function, but in case of necessity, if there is no priest available, anyone who knows the order of baptism can baptise. And if there is no man around and the child is near death, a woman can baptise if she knows the formula which Christ taught, "In the name of the Father, Son, and Holy Spirit": she sprinkles the water and says, "May (s)he be baptised." And this is a great heresy and insolent insult to the church's orders.

---

76 Pōghos Tarōnets'i, *T'ught' eranelwoyn Pōghosi Tarōnats'oy yaght'ōgh akhoyean vardapeti ǝnd dēm T'ēop'isteay Horom P'ilisop'ayin* (Epistle of the Blessed Pōghos Tarōnets'i, the Winner Adversary of the Roman Philosopher Theopistos), Constantinople, 1752, pp. 178-179: Նաեւ կանանց հրամայեն ելանել ի սուրբ խորանն Աստուծոյ, որ օտար է յԱռաքելական եւ ի Մարգարէական կանոնացն. զոր եւ ատեաց իսկ զայս Հոգին սուրբ՝ զսուրբ խորանն կռիւան առնել կանանց:

Եւ արդ՝ ահա գրեալ է յօրէնսն, եթէ Մովսէս միայն իշխէր ելանել ի գլուխ լեռին՝ եւ խոսիլ ընդ Աստուծոյ, յօրինակ այսմ Աստուածընկալ խորանիս Աստուծոյ: Եւ ամենայն բահանայքն կանգնեալ կային ի մէջ լեռինն, որ է այս եկեղեցին Քրիստոսի: Եւ ժողովուրդքն կային ի ստորոտ լեռինն, որ է արտաքին սրահ եկեղեցւոյն:

Այն լեառն՝ օրինակ էր այս սուրբ եկեղեցւոյս, եւ այսպիսի պատուիրանս՝ ի հին օրինացն եղաւ սրբութեամբ մերձենալ ի լեառն Աստուծոյ:

Իսկ ի նորումս այսպէս ասէ գիրն. եթէ Յակոբոս եղբայր տեառն՝ նա միայն իշխէր մտանել ի սրբութիւն սրբութեանց: Ի հնումն լեառն հրով վառեալ լինէր, եւ ի նորումն այս եկեղեցի, որ է ընակարան Աստուծոյ, եւ տեղի զենման՝ արեւան պատարագին Քրիստոսի:

Եւ այս է ճշմարտութիւն տնօրէնութեանն Քրիստոսի, զոր եւ սուրբ Հայրապետքն որ ի Նիկիայ ժողովեցան, զնգովս կարգեցին եւ ասացին, թէ ոչ է պարտ կանանցն ի բեմն ելանել:

Չոր եւ սուրբ Առաքեալն Պօղոս՝ արգելլոյր զգլաս կանանցն, եւ ոչ տալր նոցա թոյլ բնաւ խոսիլ յեկեղեցին: Եւ ահա դոքա հակառակ Պօղոսի եղեալ, եւ զկանայսն բեմականս արարին:

First, because such an evil heresy cannot be found in other Christian churches. Second, because God gave Adam, not the woman, the sign of this mystery at the beginning of creation when He brought the animals to Adam to give them names.

Third, because if we assume that grace had been bestowed upon the woman, why was the Mother of God, the Virgin Mary, not present at her son's baptism in Jordan?

Fourth, because if through the Apostle Philip, one of the seven deacons, the Spirit did not descend upon the eunuch until he (Philip) was carried away to Azotus by force (Acts 8:39-40), and then the Spirit descended upon the one whom he (Philip) baptised, how is it that a woman bestows the Spirit's grace through washing in water?

Fifth, because if there was the possibility for a woman, in case of need, to act as a priest, why was the virgin Nunē unable to baptise any of the Georgians when she converted them to the knowledge of God and instead, she sent a message to St Grigor, asking him for priests to baptise them?

Sixth, because if a woman can baptise in an emergency, why did St Grigor the Illuminator, who was much more honourable than a woman, not baptise any believers until he went to Caesarea and got ordained? And afterwards, thousands upon thousands, and tens upon tens of thousands came, and he baptised them in the river.

Seventh, because baptism is the priest's function, and priesthood is a service to God, and this is a service to God, neither the idolaters had this custom of offering sacrifice to their false gods by means of women, nor do any of the heathen do this. So, if it was necessary to uphold such decorum among the heathen, how much more indispensable is it in the church, which represents the true order and the law of holiness?

Eighth, considering that women have not been given the command to perform animal sacrifices, which serve as the measure of purity in matters of the flesh, how appropriate is it to permit them to approach the rite of spiritual purity?

Ninth, because baptism is the priest's function, and the priesthood is free and not subservient to anyone. The woman, on the other hand, is man's servant and foot, and for that reason, it is not right for the servant to do the master's work, as written in the canons of Nicaea that we do not permit slaves to occupy an office in the service of the church, except when freed by their masters will as in the case of Onesimus (Phm 1-25). If the holy patriarchs did not permit men in servitude to receive an ecclesiastical rank, how much greater heresy is it to allow women, to whom God said, "your desire shall be for your husband, and he shall rule over you" (Gen 3:16), to perform the office of a priest, who belongs to the class of free men, not slaves?

Tenth, because baptism is the priest's function and is performed by prayer, whereas the Apostle commands that women cover their heads during prayer because of the angels, i.e., because of the priests who are referred to as "angel" in the Scriptures. Therefore, how reprehensible is it to permit them to command and be emboldened to assume the priestly office?

Numerous other testimonies in the Holy Scriptures also reveal that such a heretical practice is false and vain.[77]

---

77   Grigor Tatʻewatsʻi, *Girkʻ Hartsʻmantsʻ* (Book of Questions), Constantinople, 1729, pp. 588-590: Դարձեալ գիտելի է, զի աստ անեն հեձնուածոդ ազգն Ֆռանկաց թէ՝ թէպէտ մկրտութիւնն գործ պահանայի է, բայց ի հարկաւոր ժամանակն թէ պահանայ ոչ լինի, ամենայն ոք որ գիտէ զնէս մկրտութեան, կարէ մկրտել: Եւ թէ այր մարդ ոչ լինի եւ տղային մերձ ի մեռանիլ լինի, կինն կարէ մկրտել թէ գիտէ զնէս բանիւն զոր Քրիստոս ուսոյց (յանուն Հօր եւ Որդւոյ եւ Հոգւոյն Սրբոյ), ցանէ զջուրն եւ ասէ՝ մկրտեալ լինի:

Նախ՝ զի այսպիսի չար աղանդս ո՛չ գտանի յայլ եկեղեցիս քրիստոնէից: Երկրորդ՝ զի զայս խորհրդոյ նշանակ ի սկզբան արարածոց Աստուած Ադամայ ետու եւ ոչ կնոջն. յորժամ էած զկենդանիսն առ Ադամայ զի անուանս դիցէ նոցա: Երրորդ, զի թէ կայր հնար որ ի ձեռն կնոջն տուեալ լինէր շնորհիք, Աստուածածին կոյսն Մարիամ ընդէ՞ր ոչ եղեւ մերձ մկրտութեան որդւոյն իւրոյ ի յորդանան: Չորրորդ, զի թէ ի ձեռն Փիլիպպոսի առաքելոյ որ էր մի յեօթանց անտի սարկաւագացն ո՛չ եղեւ իշեալ հոգին ի վերայ ներքինւոյն մինչեւ յափշտակեցաւ Յացգվտոս եւ ապա էջ հոգին ի մկրտեալն նորա, զիա՞րդ ի ձեռն կնոջ լինի տուեալ շնորհիք հոգւոյն լուացմամբ ջրոյս: Հինգերորդ, զի թէ գոյր հնար կնոջ վասն հարկին առնել զգործ պահանայի, ընդէր ո՛չ կարաց նունի կոյսն մկրտել զոք ի վրաց յորժամ դարձոյց յաստուածագիտութիւն. այլ առաքեաց առ սուրբն Գրիգոր եւ խնդրեաց քահնայս մկրտել զնոսա: Վեցերորդ, զի թէ կինն կարէ մկրտել ի հարկաւոր ժամանակի, սուրբն Գրիգոր լուսաւորիչն քանի եւս առաւել պատուական էր քան զմի կին. ընդէ՞ր ո՛չ մկրտեաց զոք ի հաւատացելոցն. մինչեւ զնաց ի Կեսարիա ձեռնադրեցաւ. եւ ապա եկեալ զհազարս հազարաց եւ զբիւրս բիւրաց մկրտեաց ի զեռն: Եօթներորդ, զի մկրտելն է գործ պահանայի. եւ քահանայութիւնն է սպասաւորութիւն Աստուծոյ. իսկ զայս սպասաւորութիւն Աստուծոյ եւ ո՛չ կոապաշտքն ունէին սովորութիւն սնոտի կռոցն ի ձեռն կանանց մատուցանել զպատարագն. զնոյն եւ ամենայն հեթանոսք առնեն: Իսկ թէ ի հեթանոսս այսպիսի պարկեշտութիւն պարտ է առնել, քանի՜ եւս առաւել յեկեղեցիս պարտ է լինիլ. որ է ճշմարիտ կարգաւորութիւն եւ սրբութեան օրէնք: Ութներորդ, զի թէ զգենումն կենդանեաց ո՛չ ունին հրամանև զենուլ ազգ կանանց որ է խոտութիւն մարմնաւոր սրբութեանց: Զիա՞րդ

Tatʻewatsʻi not only rejected women conducting baptism but also being called
to be, or acting as, a godmother within the context of baptism. He drew on
the fact that the Greek *Ekklesia, meaning "church"*, is grammatically feminine
in gender, and stated that only the church could act as the godmother, as the
"Church of the newly born." To the question, "Can a woman be a godfather?",
he replied:

> She cannot, for we say "godfather" and not "godmother" because the church
> is the godmother of the newly born. The reason for this is that a woman can-
> not be a guarantor or a witness and, hence, cannot be a godfather. And again,
> women can neither function as priests nor they can be godfathers. And not
> only that, but it is not permissible for a woman to remain in the church dur-
> ing baptism, for the Virgin Mother of the Lord was also not present at
> Christ's baptism in the Jordan, as mentioned above.[78]

պատշաճի տալ հրաման կանանց ազգի մերձենալ ի կարգ հոգեւոր սրբու-
թեան։ Իններորդ, զի մկրտութիւնն է գործ քահանայութեան. եւ քահանայութիւնն է ազատ եւ ոչ ընդ ումեք հարկի ներքոյ։ Իսկ կինն ծառայ եւ ոտք է
առն. վասն այսր հարկի ն՛չ է պարտ ծառային առնել զգործ Տեառն։ Որպէս եւ
գրեալ է ի գիրս Նիկիական կանոնացն եթէ գօառայս ի ժառանգութիւն
եկեղեցւոյ կարգել ն՛չ հրամայեմք. բայց թէ ազատեալ լիցի Տեառն կամօք.
որպէս Օնեսիմոսն այն, իսկ թէ զայր որ ընդ ծառայութեամբ է ն՛չ հրա-
մայեցին սուրբք զայ ի յաստիճան եկեղեցւոյ. քանի՞ եւս առաւել հերձնուած
մեծ է կանանց. որոյ ասաց Աստուած թէ «առ այր քո դարձ քո եւ նա տիրեսցէ
քեզ» հրաման տալ զգործ քահանայի առնել որ ազատաց եւ ոչ ծառայից։
Տասներորդ, զի մկրտութիւնն է գործ քահանայի որ աղօթիւք կատարի. իսկ
կանանց ազգին պատուիրէ առաքեալն ի ժամ աղօթիցն շուք դնել զլխոյն
վասն հրեշտակաց. այսինքն վասն քահանայից որ հրեշտակք կոչին ի գրոց,
ապա քանի՞ դատապարտութիւն է հրաման տալ նոցա եւ ի գործ քահանայութեան յանգզնի։
Են եւ այլ բազում վկայութիւնք ի գիրս սրբոց որ զայսպիսի հերձնուածս սուտ
եւ ընդունայն երեւեցուցանեն։

78 Grigor Tatʻewatsʻi, *Girkʻ Hartsʻmantsʻ*, p. 591: Հարց. Կին մարդ կարէ՞ կնքա-
    հայր լինիլ թէ ոչ։
    Պատասխանի. Ոչ կարէ. զի կնքահայր ասեմք եւ ոչ կնքամայր. զի կնքամայր
    եկեղեցին է նորածնելոցն։ Որոյ պատճառ է, զի կին երաշխաւոր եւ վկայ ն՛չ
    կարէ լինիլ վասն եւ ն՛չ կնքահայր կարէ լինիլ։ Եւ դարձեալ՝ կանանց ազգ ն՛չ
    կարէ քահանայագործէլ. եւ ն՛չ կնքահայր լինիլ։ Եւ ոչ այս միայն այլ եւ ի ժամ
    մկրտութեանն ոչ է պարտ մնալ կնոջ յեկեղեցւոջն։ Զի եւ Տիրամայր կոյսն ն՛չ
    էր ի ժամ մկրտութեան ընդ Քրիստոսի ի Յորդանան որպէս ասացաւ ի
    վերոյ։

Obviously, it is possible to argue that Tatʻewatsʻiʼs criticism here was not explicitly aimed at deaconesses but, instead, at all women who have not received ordination. In fact, we should keep in mind the fact that he did not make any reference to deaconesses, even within his interpretation of the various clerical ranks, particularly in relation to the sixth rank associated with the diaconate.[79] Yet Nersēs Lambronatsʻi, Mkhitʻar Gosh, Stepʻanos Ōrbēlean, and Smbat Sparapet all made mention of deaconesses when addressing the sixth clerical rank of the diaconate.

Concerning women being godmothers or performing baptism, the renowned *vardapet*s Yovhannēs Erznkatsʻi Pluz (*ca* 1230-1293) and Movsēs Erznkatsʻi (*ca* 1250-1323) likewise held a disapproving position. As a result, Yovhannēs Erznkatsʻi Pluz, councilled the following in his didactic treatise titled "Advice to Ordinary Christians":

> Do not make a foreigner your godfather. Do not place them within the embrace of a woman, for a godfather serves as a witness and guarantor and instructor in the faith, whereas it is not right for a woman to be either a witness, a guarantor, or a teacher.[80]

Meanwhile, Movsēs Erznkatsʻi provided commentary in regard to the heretical practices of the Marcionites within his treatise, "Refutation of Mixing Water in the Holy Eucharist of the year 1309," saying, "Women also perform ceremonies of baptism, and for this, we anathematise them."[81]

It is evident that, for these *vardapet*s, the negative attitude towards women was determined by the spirit of the time in which they lived, and it was primarily shaped by religious and ecclesiastical struggles and challenges that the contemporary Armenian clergy had to resist.

---

79   Cf. ibid., pp. 606-608.

80   See Yovhannēs Erznkatsʻi Pluz, "Xrat hasarakatsʻ Kʻristonēitsʻ" (Advice to Ordinary Christians), MS Matenadaran 1712, f. 156v: Ձայլ ազգի մի՛ առնէք կնքահայր: Ի կին մարդոյ գիրկ մի՛ դնէք, զի կանքահայր վկայ է եւ երաշխաւոր, եւ ուսուցիչ է հաւատոյն, եւ կին մարդն ոչ վկայ, ոʻչ երաշխաւոր, ոʻչ ուսուցիչ չէ պարտ որ լինի:

81   See Movsēs Erznkatsʻi, "Ĕnddimadrutʻiwn saks jroyn kharṇman i surb khorhurdn. i tʻuis hayotsʻ 558 (= 1309 CE)" (Refutation of Mixing Water in the Holy Eucharist of the year 1309), MS Matenadaran 8075, f. 132v: Այլ եւ ի կանանց լինին մկրտուսնէք, զորս նզովեʻմք: See also Ōghlugean (Manukean), Abēl, *Matenagrakan hetazōtutʻiwnner Movsēs vardapet Erznkatsʻu grakan aṙeghtsuatsi shurj* (Literary Studies regarding the Literary Mystery of *Movsēs vardapet Erznkatsʻi*), Ējmiatsin, 2001, p. 114.

However, in contrast to the intolerance mentioned above, a distinctly different perspective in favour of the ordination of deaconesses emerged within the manuscript tradition of the *Mashtots'* ritual books. In MS Venice 199 (13th century) of the Mekhitarist Library, we find a canon titled "Ordination of women deacons, who are deaconesses". There is also an additional canon with the title "Making deaconesses" in the *Mashtots'* (Cilicia, 1314) kept in the Matenadaran, the Mesrop Mashtots' Institute of Ancient Manuscripts in Yerevan.[82] The reference to the "Rank of deaconesses," found within Mashtots' manuscripts, copied in Tat'ew in the same year of 1314, among other evidence, attests to the presence of an age-old tradition regarding the ordination of deaconesses within the Armenian church. Here is the canon with the title "Ordination of women deacons, who are deaconesses":

Psalm 44, "My heart emitted the word ..."[83] is said.

Litany: "Let us implore in faith".

Then the bishop says the following prayer:

"Oh, Lord, benevolent and most merciful, all things were created by the words of Your command, and through the Incarnation of your Only Begotten Son, You have made men and women equal, for it pleased You to bestow spiritual grace not only upon men but also upon women. Likewise, at this moment, choose your female servant to serve in Your holy church and grant her grace through the Holy Spirit so that she may remain blameless and pure in her righteous deeds through the mercy of Christ, with whom glory, dominion, and honour be to You, the Father of All, and to the lifegiving and redeeming Holy Spirit, now and for ever and unto ages of ages. Amen. Our Father ..."[84]

82　See Hats'uni, *Hayuhin Patmut'ean Arjew*, p. 152.

83　This corresponds to Psalm 45 of the English Bible, which has "My heart overflows with a goodly theme ...".

84　See MS Matenadaran 907, scribe – Erinē (written in cipher), folios 309v-310r:
Կանոն ձեռնադրութեան սարկաւագ կանանց, որ են սարկաւագուհիք:
Ասի Սաղմոս. ԽԴ. Բղխեացէ սիրտ իմ զպատգամս քո բարիս:
Քարոզ. Խնդրեսցուք հաւատով:

Եւ ասէ զաղաւթս զայս. Աստուած բարերար եւ բազմագուղ, որ զամենայն արարեր բանիւ հրամանի քո, եւ ի ձեռն մարմնաւոր տնտեսութեան Միածնիդ քում հաւասարեցուցեր զարուն եւ զէգն որպէս հաճոյ թուեցաւ քեզ ոչ միայն արանց այլ եւ կանանց տալ շնորհս հոգեւորս: Նոյնպէս եւ այժմ ընտրեա զաղախին քո առ ի պաշտաւն պիտոյից եկեղեցւոյ քո սրբոյ եւ տուր նմա շնորհս ի Հոգւոյդ Սրբոյ, զի պահեսցէ զսա ամբիծ եւ անարատ ի գործս

This canon regarding the ordination of deaconesses is also found in the following manuscripts of the Mersop Mashtots' Matenadaran:

> MS 907, ff. 309v-310r (17ᵗʰ c.)
> MS 953, ff. 114r-115r (1656)
> MS 954, f. 80v (16ᵗʰ c.)
> MS 960, f. 243v (1498)
> MS 962, f. 62r (1530)
> MS 970, f. 69r (16ᵗʰ c.)
> MS 998, ff. 226v-227v (1546)
> MS 2787, ff. 168r-168v (1314)
> MS 3508, ff. 160r-160v (1434)
> MS 4195, f. 305v. (1321)
> MS 4363, ff. 288v-289r (16ᵗʰ c.)
> MS 4961, ff. 251r-251v (15ᵗʰ c.)
> MS 5153, f. 182v (16ᵗʰ c.)
> MS 6450, ff. 160r-160v (1443)[85]

Our oldest surviving manuscripts containing the canon regarding the ordination of deaconesses date back to the 13ᵗʰ and 14ᵗʰ centuries, as found in MS Venice 199 and MS Matenadaran 2787. Based on this evidence, it could be inferred that this canon was included in the Mashtots' ritual book in the ninth century. This likely occurred during the initial compilation of the Mashtots' by Catholicos Mashtots' I Eghivardets'i between 897-898.[86]

արդարութեան ողորմութեամբ Քրիստոսի քո: Ընդ որում քեզ Հաւր ամենակալի կենդանարար եւ ազատիչ Սուրբ Հոգւոյդ վայելէ փառք, իշխանութիւն
եւ պատիւ այժմ եւ միշտ եւ յաւիտեանս յաւիտենից. Ամէն. Հայր մեր ... See
also MS 237 of the National Library (Galata) (*Loys*, Constantinople, 1906, p.
1200).

85 The late Gēorg Tēr-Vardanean, the former senior curator of the Matenadaran,
brought this data to my attention, for which I am most grateful.

86 The first redaction of the ritual book *Mashtots'* is ascribed to the Catholicos
Mashtots' I Eghivardets'i, whose name the compilation bears. This is attested by
historian Kirakos Gandzakets'i: "He (i.e. Mashtots' Eghivardets'i) compiled the
book which is called Mashtots' after his name, collecting all the set prayers and
readings adjusting them together with his own additions; it contains within itself
all the orders of the Christian faith"; Սա կարգեաց զգիրսն որ ըստ իւր ան-
ուանն Մաշտոց կոչի, ժողովեալ զամենայն կարգեալ աղօթս եւ զընթերց-
ուածս ի միասին յարմարեալ յաւելուածով յիւրմէ, որ ունի յինքեան զամենայն կարգս հաւատոյ քրիստոնէութեան: (see Kirakos Gandzakets'i, *Kirakos
vardapeti Gandzakets'woy hamaṛōt patmut'iwn i srboy Grigorē yawurs iwr lusabaneal* (A Brief History from St Grigor until His Days Explained), Venice, 1865,

Based on this, we can say it is possible that in the ninth century, the Armenian Church already demonstrated exceptional and unparalleled open-mindedness in relation to granting women clerical authority. And although this was not prescriptive, it was unquestionably regarded as a component of tradition. The following words from the ordination prayer exemplify the spirit of the era: "through the Incarnation of your Only Begotten Son, You *have made* men and women *equal,* for it pleased You to *bestow spiritual grace not only upon men but also upon women."* [87]

This predates the motto of the French Revolution, "Liberté, Égalité, Fraternité," by almost a thousand years, as well as the demands of the feminist movement of the twentieth century.

This statement was exemplified thanks to the prominent sixteenth-century churchman, poet, and manuscript illustrator, Catholicos Grigoris Aght'amarts'i (1480-1544). He portrayed the image of a saintly deaconess in the right margin of folio 62r of a *Mashtots'*, MS Matenadaran 962, which was copied in Archēsh monastery in 1530 and which contains the exact same canon "Ordination of women deacons, who are deaconesses". [88] The deaconess is depicted, not in a daunting, burqa-like black vestment, but with an uncovered face and a headscarf adorned with a cross. It can be surmised that Grigoris Aght'amarts'i had likely observed or was familiar with real deaconesses residing in various Armenian communities and monasteries. As a result, he likely held no negative biases nor was constrained by negative preconceptions, since he painted an Armenian deaconess with a radiant countenance next to the noted canon. The significance of this testimony lies in the fact that, within the incense-filled sanctuary of Archēsh monastery in 1530, as he illustrated the *Mashtots'* manuscript, Grigoris Aght'amarts'i had already held the position of an elected Catholicos since 1512. It is difficult to envision that the highest-ranking servant of the Armenian church would openly exhibit such liberal thinking without having a high degree of confidence in the existence of a sacred tradition of deaconesses within the heart of his Mother and Sacred Church.

---

p. 45). See also Archbishop Maghak'ia Ōrmanean, *Azgapatum* (National History), Vol. I, Constantinople, 1913, cols. 1016-1018).

87   Emphasis mine.

88   See the figures below. I would like to express my heartfelt gratitude to Armine Melkonyan, a senior researcher at the Mesrop Mashtots' Matenadaran, for bringing this illustration to my attention.

An Armenian deaconess, according to the miniature by Catholicos Grigoris Aghtʿamartsʿi. MS Matenadaran 962, f. 62r, Mashtotsʿ, scribe – Yovhannēs, illustrator – Catholicos Grigoris Aghtʿamartsʿi, place – Archēsh, year – 1530.

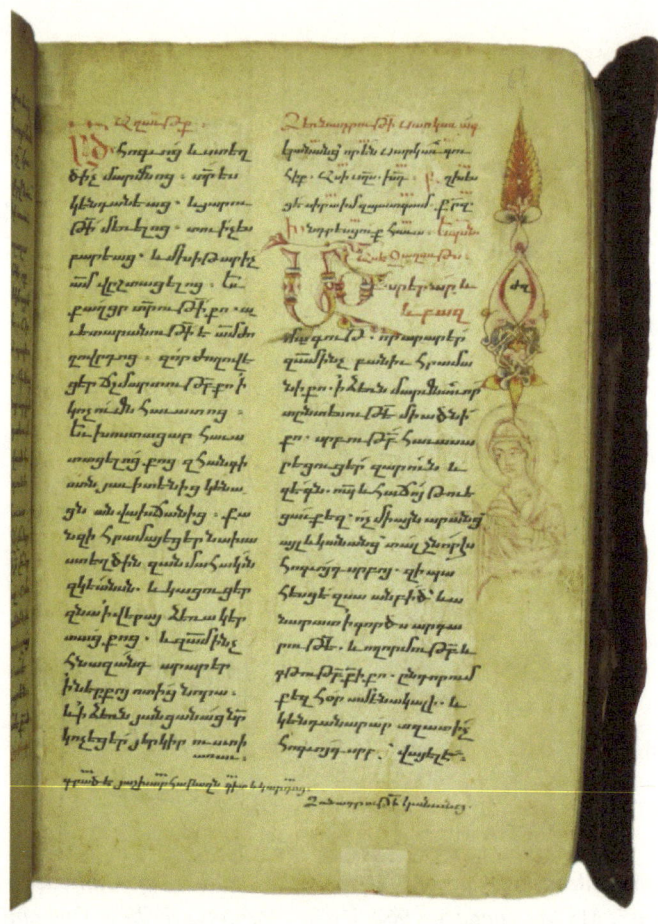

Canon "Ordination of women deacons, who are deaconesses", MS Matenadaran 962, f. 62r, Mashtots', scribe – Yovhannēs, illustrator – Catholicos Grigoris Aght'a-marts'i, place – Archēsh, year – 1530.

Revival of the Female Diaconate in the 17th Century

Despite the dire political situation in Armenia in the 17th century, where, the land and its people were suffering under the oppressive Persian rule, and the Catholicos's throne in Ějmiatsin had become a subject of contention among competing Catholicoi, this century is still regarded as a period of spiritual and cultural awakening in our history. It is during this challenging historical period that Armenian monasticism experienced a revival, especially in the land of Siwnik', thanks to the tremendous efforts of *vardapet*s such as Movsēs III Tat'ewats'i, Pōghos Mokats'i, Kirakos Pontats'i, and Sargis Paronter.[89]

Amid this widespread spiritual and cultural awakening, not only were Armenian male monasteries reorganised, but several convents were also established in Siwnik'. In his highly influential and voluminous treatise *Sisakan*, Fr Ghewond Alishan mentioned nunneries alongside male monasteries as part of the monastic establishments in the Siwnik' region: "The convent of the Mother of God in Halidzor, the convent of the Mother of God in Shinaher, the convent of the Mother of God in Noratunk', the convent of Ilkevank', the convent of Kot', the convent of Shorot'" and so on.[90]

In this list, it is especially worth noting the convents of Shenher (Shinuhayr) and Shorot', significant for the number of nuns who lived in each, and for their prolific manuscript production. Below are specific details from the previously mentioned work concerning the two convents:

> Shnher, which is not only larger than Halis and Khot but also surpasses all the villages in the region, has been the second village of Dzoraget since ancient times and remains as such today. This is perhaps the reason why some people interpret it in their writings as Shinahayr or Shinuhayr, while others invert the word as Hayrashen [...]. Near Shnher, one could find the grand convent of the Holy Mother of God sprawling across a high plateau west of

---

89 See Aṛak'el Davrizhets'i, *Patmut'iwn Aṛak'el Vardapeti Dawrizhets'woy* (History of the Vardapet Aṛak'el Davrizhets'i), Vagharshapat, 1896, pp. 249-314. See also Archbishop Maghak'ia Ōrmanean, *Azgapatum* (National History), Vol. II, Constantinople, 1914, cols. 2318-2320, 2335-2339, 2342-2350, 2362-2366, 2385-2389, 2399-2422 and Akinean, Nersēs, *Movsēs ÎII Tat'ewats'i Hayots' Kat'oghikosn ew ir zhamanakě: Npast mě Hayots' ekeghets'woy patmut'ean 1577-1633 shrjani hamar* (Catholicos Movsēs III Tat'ewats'i and His Time: A Contribution to Armenian Ecclesiastical History for the Period 1577-1633), Vienna, 1936.

90 Alishan, *Sisakan: Teghagrut'iwn Siwneats'ashkharhi*, pp. 21-22.

Halidzor. Its church and the fortified walls with cell sections, constructed in 1676 during the reign of Catholicos Yakob IV, still stand to this day [...] as evident from the inscription on the wall of the church apse.[91]

This house of refuge was built by the grace of the Holy Spirit in the year 1125 (= 1676 CE), during the reign of His Holiness Lord Yakob.[92]

Furthermore, there is an inscription on the arch commemorating the builder, Azri or Azaria, dated 1676:

Inspired by the Holy Spirit, I, Azri, the most sinful *mahtēsi*[93] from the plain of Agulis, came to the gathering place of women and was tasked to build this church, its precincts, and the holy abodes. It had been warm for 30 days in the year 1676 since the birth of the Saviour.[94]

The inscription located on the upper section of the convent's door unequivocally indicates the same year:

In the year 1676 of our Lord Jesus Christ, this church was constructed through the means of us, the handmaidens, eighty in number, who have gathered here in this monastery. Years after the construction of this house, some of us arose and went to the land of Agulis, and having come here, with great labour and their fairly earned assets, he built this church. He commenced on 4 April and completed it on 8 September, and for this reason, I implore you, sisters and virgins who will come after us, [to remember] the service of our brother ...[95]

Aside from the previously mentioned inscriptions, we also possess a collection of written sources preserved in the form of colophons of manuscripts, which were copied by the nun scribes residing in the same Shenher convent. It should be mentioned that the history of our scribal tradition also includes

---

91 Ibid., p. 258. In this regard, see also Arzumanyan, M. V. et al (eds.), *Haykakan Sovetakan Hanragitaran* (Soviet Armenian Encyclopaedia), Vol. VIII, Yerevan, 1982, p. 508: "To the south of the village, at the edge of the Vorotan valley, lies a convent complex consisting of a church, *gawit'*, refectory, and cells enclosed by a wall. The church of the Holy Mother of God was constructed in 1676."

92 Alishan, *Sisakan: Teghagrut'iwn Siwneats'ashkharhi*, p. 258. The convent's construction date, 1676, suggests that it was built during the reign of Catholicos Yakob IV Jughayets'i.

93 *Mahtēsi* (*mahdasi*) was the title bestowed upon those embarking on pilgrimages to Jerusalem, implying that such journeys were fraught with perils arising from insecure routes, various diseases, or natural disasters during that period.

94 Ibid., p. 259.

95 Ibid.

women scribes: many virtuous nuns dedicated themselves to the service of Armenian culture and the advancement of the scribal art.[96]

We find the following information about the convent in the colophon of MS Matenadaran 1455, authored by the nun Mariam:

> [...] upon the completion and fulfilment of the twenty-second jubilee and on the same date according to the Japhetic calendar (i.e. year 1651) this manu-script [...] which was called *Oskepʻorik* was written in ink by the hand of a feeble, worthless, falsely named Mariam, believer in name only and virgin, but extremely weak in achieving results and in action [...] under the auspices of the most blessed Holy Mother of God and within the holy convent called Shēnher, inhabited by angels, amid a multitude of nuns who wore hairshirts ...[97]

The phrase "amid a multitude of nuns who wore hairshirts" suggests that at least tens of nuns likely resided in the Shenher convent. We saw above that this significant count is corroborated by the inscription made on the entrance door of the building, mentioning "eighty in number". However, nearly six decades after the convent's establishment, in 1735, Catholicos Abraham III Kretatsʻi, quite possibly during a pastoral visit to the Shenher convent, ob-served a decline in its former glory and, with sadness, left behind the subse-quent testimony:

96　See Pogharyan, Norayr, "Hay grchʻuhiner" (Armenian Women Scribes), *Sion*, IV-V, 1954, pp. 133-134.

97　MS Matenadaran 1455, ff. 506v-506r (1673): [...] Ի լրումն քառներորդ երկրորդ յոբելինին եւ ի նոյնքան թիւս ժամանելոյ Յաբեթական տոհմիս տոմարի (1651) մելանագրեցաւ մատեանս [...] որ կոչի Ոսկեփորիկ: Զեռամբ տկար եւ ապիկար՝ սուտանունն Մարիամ հաւատ[աւ]որ եւ կուսան կոչեցեալ ան-ուամբ եւեթ, այլ արդեամբ եւ գործով յոյժ տկարացեալ [...] ընդ հովանեաւ ամենօրհնեալ Սուրբ Աստուածածանիս եւ հրեշտակաբնակ Սուրբ մենաս-տանիս Շէնհէր կոչեցելոյ: Ի մէջ բազմահոյլ եւ խարազնազգեստ կուսանաց ... See also MS Matenadaran 4088, copied in Shēnher by a woman scribe named Erinē, ff. 256r-257r: Արդ, շնորհիւ բարերարին սկսա[յ] եւ ողորմութեամբ նո-րին կատարեցի ի թուարկութեանս Հայոց ՌՃԻ եւ Բ [...] գրեցաւ սա որ կոչի Ժամագիրք եւ ատենի ի յանապատս Շինհէրու ի դուռն Սուրբ Աստուա-ծածնին ("Now, by the grace of the Benevolent One I began and with His mercy completed [this text] in the year 1122 of the Armenian Era (= 1673) [...] this [text] which is called *Zhamagirkʻ Ateni* (Liturgical Brevary) was copied in the convent of Shinhēr at the door of the Holy Mother of God").

This place, formerly inhabited by over 150 virgins, now only harboured 12 penitents, and even they seemed lost and despondent [...]. I said words of encouragement to the penitents and [noted] all the lacking church essentials such as books, a measure of cloth, chalice and cross, and also *kataghunik*[98], where men would stand when they came on a visit. The hermitage was dilapidated and in ruins. I instructed them to locate a carpenter, procure the necessary timber and planks, and I covered the costs of the materials. I then directed the master carpenter to construct it promptly, and I departed. And [...] I purchased and dispatched them all the vessels I could find in the village of Tatʻew. And since they lacked flour for bread, I directed them to provide some wheat from the monastery to people in need.[99]

The convent of Shoṛotʻ, meanwhile, is among the nunneries that also emerged in the 17ᵗʰ century as a result of the broader spiritual and cultural revival. The village of Shoṛot,ʻ or Shuṛutʻ, of the Ernjak province (in Nakhijevan) is mentioned in historical sources from the 13ᵗʰ century. In the 17ᵗʰ century, it was already depicted as having "thrived through wealth and trade, construction and renovation of churches".[100] Before becoming the Catholicos (1629-1639), Movsēs III Tatʻevatsʻi also visited this area with his colleague, the *vardapet* Pōghos Mokatsʻi and established a school "so that boys from the surrounding villages will assemble there and be provided with education".[101] As we can observe, in the Armenian tradition, education was not restricted to men but was also available for women, albeit in a separate environment within the confines of a convent. The following written references have been preserved regarding the Shoṛotʻ convent:

O holy fathers, brothers, and thoughtful readers, when you encounter this holy book, by reading or just seeing it, may you remember in your virtuous prayers the sinful Aristakēs, falsely named so, the waster of the Word, who hails from the land of Bznunikʻ, from the province of Khlatʻ, and now I am wandering around in Nakhijevan, far from home. Also [remember] my sister Margarit, the blessed nun, who copied not only this but has laboured on

---

98 From the Greek word καταγώγιον, which means "lodging, resting place", which must have been borrowed into Armenian. It refers to the section of the convent that men could enter for some business without directly interacting with the nuns. In Shenher, which was a women's monastery, the church's *kataghunik*ʻ was a place from where men visiting the convent could secretly observe the nuns pray (see Alishan, *Sisakan: Teghagrutʻiwn Siwneatsʻ ashkharhi*, p. 260).

99 Ibid., pp. 259-260.

100 Ibid.

101 Ibid., p. 351.

many writings. Because our mother passed away when she was one year old, she was nurtured in the hermitage among the nuns. When she was of age, she began the scribal art and continued until old age, receiving nothing [for her work], for she did everything for the glory of God, and may she be rewarded for her labours from Him. She also devoted considerable effort to the wretched me, both in writing letters and attending to other matters for years, and she was instrumental in delivering me from the world and ensuring my commitment to my professional calling. Albeit deceived by sin and in a state of privation, I implore Christ with my sinful mouth to reward her according to her kindnesses and, after this life, include her in the rank of the wise virgins. Amen.[102]

[...] And now I, Aristakēs, the last among the scholars and the unruly one among the disciplined, poor in worldly possessions and exiled from my homeland, servant of the Word by a divine calling, lacking in deeds and void of virtues, misled by sin, longed with fervent love and passionate desire for this holy book which is a compilation of the good tidings of the Holy Gospels of Matthew and John, as a remedy for my irremediable soul and a tiller for my shipwrecked life and gave it to my sister Margarit to copy in the region of Ernjak in the convent of Shoṙotʿ, under the auspices of the Holy Mother of God, in the year of the Armenian Era 1120 (= 1671 CE).[103]

---

102 MS Matenadaran 9240, f. 14v (1671): Ով սրբազան հարք եւ եղբարք եւ խոհեմ ընթերցողք. յորժամ հանդիպիք սբ. զրոյս ընթեռնելով եւ կամ հարեւանցի տեսանելով, յիշեսջիք ի մաքրափայլ յաղօթս ձեր զմեղսամած պիտականուն Արիստակէս, բանի վատնողս, որ եմ աշխարհաւ Բզնունեաց, ի նահանգէն Դլապայ, եւ այժմ եմ պանդուխտ ի յերկիրս Նախիջեւանու. նաեւ զերանուհի կուսակրօն հարազատ քրոյն իմ ՄԱՐԳԱՐԻՏ, զծող տառս եւ ոչ այս միայն այլ եւ բազում գրեանս աշխատեալ. քանզի մի ամաց լեալ, մայրն վախ-ճանեալ եւ նա յանապատս սնեալ ի մէջ կուսանաց եւ յորժամ յարբունս հասեալ, սկիզբն արարեալ գրչութեան արուեստի, մինչեւ ի ծերութեան ժամանակի, եւ ոչինչ ստացեալ, այլ զամենայն ի փառս Աստուծոյ եւ ի նմանէ ընկայցի վարձս վաստակոց իւրոց եւ ի վերայ հիքոյս այս բազում աշ-խատեցաւ, թէ՛ զիր գրելով եւ թէ այլքն ամովք, որ եղեւ պատճառ յաշխարհէ կորզելոյ եւ ի կարգ կոչմանն պահելով, թէպէտ զարածեալս մեղօք, յետնեալ զտայ, խնդրեմ մեղապարտ բերանովս, որ ըստ իւր երախտեացն Քրիստոս լիցի վարձահատոյց եւ յետ այստեացս ընդ իմաստուն սբ. Կուսանացն դա-սասկէ. ամէն:

103 Ibid., ff. 184r-185r: Եւ արդ ես վերջինս բանասիրաց եւ անկարգս ի կար-գաւորաց, աղքատ յնչեղեաց, վտարանդիս ի հայրենեաց Արիստակէս, վե-րերեւլոյն կոչմամբ բանի սպասաւոր, դատարկ ի գործոյն եւ թափուր ի բար-եաց, զառածեալս մեղօք, ջերմեռանդ սիրով եւ տարփատենչ յօժարութեամբ ցանկացայ սբ. զրոյս, որ է ալետաբեր քաղուածոյ սբ. Աւետարանին զլխոյն

At the end of the same manuscript, another scribe, likely a contemporary, composed the following encomium to the commendable virgin:

> [...] We should also say, "[Lord], have mercy" on Margarit, the same sister [of Aristakēs],
> For she was a penitent virgin, diligent in work and never experiencing boredom,
> For she wrote many books by hand and left them to the Armenian Church.
> For she grew very old in labours, having lived a long life,
> May the Lord grant her some of His remedy and deem her worthy of His kingdom.
> You, Margarit,[104] aged mother, yearn for the clay of death,
> In this world, you have seen much sorrow, even more from your own family,
> Devoted to the toil of copying, a glint of light slipped from your eyes,
> May the Lord of remedies reward you along with the wise virgins. And to Him be glory always, for ever, in the past, the present, and the future.[105]

In a colophon of another miscellanious manuscript copied in 1669 by a woman scribe, we read:

> Now, this holy book was copied in the year 1118 of the Armenian Era (= 1669), during the patriarchate of His Holiness Catholicos Lord Yakob in the Holy See of Ējmiatsin and the leadership of the great teacher Yesayi in our region, in the town of Shōṛōtʻ of the province of Ernjak, under the auspices of the Holy Mother of God and the Saint Illuminator, by the hand of Margarit, a soul entangled in sin, shaken by life, and perishing in the depths of unrighteousness, full of evil in spirit ...[106]

Մատթէոսի եւ Յովհաննու, եւ անճարակ հոգոյ իմոյ ճար. եւ նաւաբեկեալ կենաց իմոյ դեկ ապաշինութեան ստացայ սուրբ զիրքս եւ եռու գրել զայս հարագատ բերն իմոյ ՄԱՐԳԱՐՏԻ, ի յերկիրս Երնջակայ, ի կուսաստանն ՃՕՌՕԹՈՒ, ընդ հովանեաւ սբ. Աստուածածնին, ի թվահաշուութեան ազգիս արամեան Ռ.Ձ. եւ Ի: A similar testimony is also found on f. 345v of the manuscript.

104 This could also be a reference to *margarit* = pearl.

105 Ibid., ff. 346v-347r.

106 MS Matenadaran 1735, f. 365r: Արդ, գրեցաւ սուրբ զիրքս ի թուականութեանս Հայոց ՌՃԺԲ (1669)-ի, ի հայրապետութեան Սուրբ Աթոռոյն Էջմիածնի տեառն Յակոբայ սրբազան կաթողիկոսի, ի յառաջնորդութեան մերոյս նահանգի՝ եսայեալ բազ րաբունապետի, ի յերկիրս Երնջակ, ի գեողաքաղաքս Ճօռօթ, ընդ հովանեաւ, Սուրբ Աստուածածնիս եւ Սուրբ Լուսաւորչին ձեռամբ գրեալ ոգոյ, մեղօք վարանեալ, կենօք տատանեալ եւ ի խորս անօրէնութեան կործանեալ շառաւայից հոգով՝ Մարգարտի ...:

It is immensely heartening to see that within the ranks of prominent figures of Armenian culture, there were devout virgins of Christ who held their faith with unwavering conviction. These women, for the salvation of their souls, dedicated themselves not only to the introspective prayers and arduous monastic labour to sustain their daily lives, but at the same time also made significant contributions to the rich heritage of Armenian culture. Indeed, in an interesting article from 2021, Tamara Minasyan wrote:

> In Artsakh, there were also women scribes: the nuns Gayanē, Katarine, and Varvara, of whom only few manuscripts have reached us. In the 17ᵗʰ century, the female hermitage of the Awetaranots borough, established in the fifth century by King Vachʻē II, where he copied a Gospel, became a prominent scriptorium and was associated with Gayanē, the daughter of Varanda's *melikʻ* Huseyn. We possess a *Mashtotsʻ* manuscript from 1641 (MS Matenadaran 2404), which was not only copied but also illustrated by Gayanē. Gayanē also illustrated a Gospel manuscript copied by Katarine in 1650 in Tʻaghavard, which is now in the repository of ancient manuscripts in Vienna (MS Vienna 931). Whereas Varvara was active in Dadivankʻ.[107]

---

107 See Minasyan, Tamara, "Artsakhi dzeṛagrakan zhaṛangutʻyunĕ" (The Manuscript Tradition of Artsakh), in *Das armenische Kulturerbe in Berg-Karabach/Arzach und die* Deutschen, Martin Tamcke et al (eds.), Göttingen, 2021, pp. 47-60; p. 53. In the 20ᵗʰ century, there still were deaconesses in Shushi, one of whom was the deaconess Gayanē Vardapetyan, who was martyred in July-August of 1906 during the massacres of the Armenian population of the city by the Azeri slaughterers (see Mikʻaelyan, Davitʻ, "Averum en moṛatsʻutʻyunitsʻ pʻrkvats verjin nshkharnerĕ: Inchʻ en hushum Shushii haykakan gerezmanotsʻi vimagir ardzanagrutʻyunnerĕ" (They are destroying the last remnants saved from oblivion: What do the inscriptions from the Armenian cemetery of Shushi relate?), *Hayastani Hanrapetutʻyun*, 11 September, 2021. <https://hhpress.am/taratsashrjan/2021/5532/>, accessed on 16 January 2024. After this bloody massacre, the devastated nunnery of Shushi was closed, and the nun Nunē Sargsyan and the 90-year-old abbess of the convent Hṛipʻsimē, who survived the slaughter, fled to foreign lands and found refuge under the skies of Ashkhabad. In 1925, the nun Nunē penned a heart-wrenching letter to Catholicos Gēorg V, in which she described their dire situation: "As a result of external evil and internal arrogance, along with many provinces of Armenia, beautiful Shushi and in it our monastery-hermitage were destroyed. Alongside the survivors of the massacre, Abbess Hṛipʻsimē and I, two virgins, fled almost naked and sought refuge in the city of Paltaratskʻ (Ashkhabad) in the Transcaspian region. For six years, we lived with meagre provisions and scant clothing, relying on the mercy of acquaintances as we moved from door to door, but we did not reach out to You, the Mother of the clergy,

In 1895, in Baku, Bishop Makar Barkhutareants' published a compilation of observational findings derived from his research expedition to his native Artsakh, titled "Artsakh". With reference to the monastery of Dati-Bēkants, he wrote:

> Due to the absence of a spring or potable water source in this village, the archdeaconess and most humble nun P'ep'ronĕ, of the Khubean Mēlik'-Bēklareants' family, using her personal funds, had potable water brought in clay pipes from the mountain to the village, where it was bifurcated, with one branch directed towards the church for communal use, and the other extending to the yard of the esteemed T'alish-bēk Mēlik'-Bēklareants'. At the church, there is an inscription on the water fountain: "I, nun archdeaconess P'ep'ronĕ, of the Khubean Mēlik'-Bēklareants' family, built the spring in the village of Kharkhap'ut' (Khrkhap'or) with my personal funds as a memorial for myself and my deceased parents and sisters and brothers, on 1 March 1893."[108]

In the same publication, the author made a reference to the Anapat Kusanats' (Virgins Hermitage) of Artsakh, stating:

> You, the guardian Patriarch, hoping that You might become interested in your lost daughters.
>
> However, due to your busy schedule, You have forgotten us until now, as we have reached a point where we can no longer endure the dishonourable state of begging and hunger, and we find it necessary to bring our existence and situation to Your attention. The decrepit nun Hrip'simē, about 90 years old, sent me to report to You and tell You that since childhood, we, as members of the clergy, have dedicated our entire lives to the monastic path, and today we find ourselves on the brink of starvation. Thanks to Your high rank, You keep, sustain, and take care of the Ējmiatsin congregation: kindly extend Your benevolence to us as well. We have not been stepchildren of the Armenian Church. Now, when our country is resurrected from the ruins by the efforts of the Soviet government, experiencing economic growth, and both the congregation of Holy Ējmiatsin and the people benefit from this collective economic prosperity, please do not allow two deserving virgins like us to starve outside the monasteries and in foreign lands.
>
> We ask you, Your Holiness, either to grant us a place to stay and ensure our sustenance until our passing, or to deliver Your decisive word, which I will then convey to the nun Hrip'simē, and we will take care of our fate" (see the online article by Heghine Mkrtch'yan, "Kusanats' lk'vats anapatneri sarkavaguhinerĕ" (The Deaconesses of Abandoned Female Hermitages), Published 24 Febr. 2016, <https://ter-hambardzum.net/կուսանաց-լքված-անապատների-սարկավագո/>, accessed on 16 January 2024.

108 Barkhutareants', Makar, *Artsakh*, Bagu, 1895, p. 244.

It is founded on the elevated ground (almost midway between the Meghri and Nor-t'agh churches), arcaded, without columns, featuring two doors from the southern and western sides, nine windows and one three-storeyed bell house that shares a common wall with the southern side. The length of the temple is 20 metres, the width 9 metres and 45 centimetres.

On the stone lintel above the southern door:

"This holy church was built in the name of the Holy Mother of God through the skilled hands and labour of the nun Hṛip'simē, with the assistance of her three brothers, Israēl, Astuatsatur, and Petros Grigorean Bahadureants, in the year 1816." The same assiduous nun Hṛip'simē had the bell tower built without receiving any assistance.

There is a Gospel manuscript in the hermitage in fair condition, written on paper and illustrated. From the colophon:

"The faithful landlord Yakovb and his father, *paron* Grigor, are the ones who purchased this [manuscript] through their fairly earned assets [...] And now, I, Mkrtich' *abegha*, the last from among the scribes and the unworthy one from among the clergymen [...] received an order from the Apostolic Word that gives commandments [...] This holy Gospel was copied in the holy congregation called the Saln Hermitage, where God lives and angels walk, under the auspices of the Holy Mother of God and Saint Karapet [...] during the patriarchate of the Catholicos Lord Sargis, in the year 934 (= 1485) of the Armenian Era by the hand of [...] *abegha*." On the side of the Gospel, there is a note: "This holy Gospel is a memorial for the abbess of the convent of the Virgins of Shushi Vaṛvaṛa Bahat'reants', in the year 1888, on 31 of the eight month in Shushi."

The hermitage has an honest and diligent caretaker, a trustee abbess, three deaconesses, and one novice nun.[109]

In the nunnery of Shoṛot', there were also other women scribes who, like the nun Margarit, excelled in the Armenian scribal tradition, leaving behind a commendable legacy. Among many, were the nun Goharinē, who copied Grigor Narekats'i's prayer book in 1687-1688, and the nun Shushan, who copied Khorenats'i and Eghishē[110]. We deem it unnecessary to quote their

---

109 Ibid., pp. 148-149.
110 Renowned literary figures from the fifth century, both of them enjoyed an outstanding reputation, especially among Armenians.

colophons here one by one;[111] however, for the present material, the colophon of the MS Matenadaran 39, *Miscellany*, may be interesting, for the female scribe has added her title in front of her name using a ligature, which is, "Ustianē SARKAWAG" (Ustianē the deacon). Based on this information and the earlier-mentioned details, we can draw the following conclusions:

i.   There were deaconesses in the Armenian convents in the 17th–18th centuries.

ii.   The tradition of conferring the rank of deaconess upon women was not an innovation of those centuries, but it was undoubtedly a continuation of a long-established custom in the Armenian Church.

iii. Above, we observed that following the example of Abraham III Kretats'i, starting with Movsēs III Tat'evats'i, our Catholicoi did not consider the existence of not only the female convents but also the deaconesses, to be against the creed of the church. On the contrary, they directly encouraged them and supported them flourishing in their religious calling.

---

111 Alishan, *Sisakan: Teghagrut'iwn Siwneats'ashkharhi*, pp. 353-354. See also Tsovakan, Nersēs, "Hay Grch'uhiner" (Armenian Women Scribes), *Sion*, IV-V, 1954, pp. 133-134.

Vestments of Deaconesses

The first evidence concerning the vestments of Armenian deaconesses dates back to the 12th century. All authors invariably mention a small metallic cross hanging from their forehead and a stole worn over the right shoulder. We can read the following in Mkhit'ar Gosh regarding this:

> "Their habit is that common to all believers[112], save a cross is worn on the forehead, and they have a stole hanging down on the right side."[113]

Smbat Sparapet[114] and Stepanos Ōrbēlean[115] provide virtually identical information. In photographs from a later period, specifically the 19th and 20th centuries, we can observe a deaconess attired in a robe with a white veil that extends to the ground.

---

112 According to the *Nor Baṛgirk' Haykazean Lezui* (vol. II, p. 78), *hawatawor* ("believer") may refer to "a virgin, young lady or woman who has dedicated herself to God with faith and steadfastness; nun". The historical connection between the position of the believers in our church and deaconesses requires additional scholarly attention.

113 Thomson, *Datastanagirk' of Mxit'ar Goš*, p. 278; Mkhit'ar Gosh, *Girk' Datastani*, p. 137: Սբեմ է նոցա ամենայն ինչ հաւատաւորաց, բայց ի ճակատն խաչ լինի, եւ բուշկեն ի յաջմէ կողմանէ ի կախ ունելով: See also Hats'uni, Vardan, *Patmut'iwn hin hay tarazin* (History of the Ancient Armenian Dress), Venice, 1923, pp. 440-441.

114 See above, note 71; Hats'uni, *Patmut'iwn hin hay tarazin*, pp. 440-441.

115 See above, note 73; Hats'uni, *Patmut'iwn hin hay tarazin*, pp. 440-441.

A stole adorned with golden needlework. It belonged to the deaconesses of the Saint Step'anos monastery of Tbilisi. Saint Gēorg Church, Tbilisi.

An Armenian deaconess in liturgical vestments.[116]

116 Liturgical vestments of a deaconess serving in the Armenian Church in Constantinople (19th century). She wears an orarion and a fine silver-wrought veil, and holds a flabellum in her hand. The photograph was taken in front of the altar of the Armenian Apostolic Church of St Sarkis in Tehran to depict the Armenian deaconess from Constantinople. However, it appears that the authors of the book have conflated the deaconesses of Tiflis with those of Constantinople. See *The Costumes of Armenian Women,* by Gregory Lima, Hay Kin Society of Tehran, published by International Communicators, Tehran, Iran, 1974, p. 80 <https://commons.wikiedia.org/wiki/File:%D5%8D%D5%A1%D6%80%D5%AF%D5%A1%D6%82%D5%A1%D5%A3%D5%B8%D6%82%D5%B0%D5%AB.jpg>.

Armenian Nunneries Outside the Borders of Armenia

Female Monasteries of Virtuous Armenian Women and the Nunnery of St Hṛipʻsimian Virgins in Poland in 16th-17th Centuries

In 2022, in Krakow, the publishing house Księgarnia Akademicka issued an interesting volume titled *Niewiasty z Pastorałami* (Women with Crosiers), which also had the following subtitle: *Portrety Ksień Klasztoru Benedyktynek Ormiańskich we Lwowie: Historia, Konteksty, Konserwacja* (Portraits of the Abbesses of the Armenian Benedictine Monastery in Lwów: History, Contexts, Conservation).[117] This publication captured our attention when we read Dr Ara Sayegh's valuable review of this material in the Armenian press in 2023.[118] Additionally, the summary of this volume from its publishers provides the following information:

> There are two reasons why the history of the Armenian nunnery in Lwów in the Kingdom of Poland (now Lviv in Ukraine) is special. The first is the uniqueness of the forms of Armenian female monasticism, the second is the traditional role of women according to Armenian customs. Among Polish Armenians, in Kamieniec Podolski (Kam'yanets'-Podil's'kyi), Jazłowiec (Yazlovets), and Lwów (Lviv), the idea of community organized by women was not easy to reconcile with the principle of male domination in family life, which was in force among Armenian immigrants to an incomparably higher degree than it was in Polish society. The first Armenian nuns in Poland were, therefore, entirely subordinate to the authority of the elders of an ethnic commune, who even usurped the right to consent to the accession of new candidates. Even deaconesses—which the Armenian Church, unlike other churches, retained from the times of early Christianity—did not gain an exceptional position (only two Armenian deaconesses are known from the territory of the Kingdom of Poland, both from the end of the 17th century).[119]

---

117 Andrzej A. Zięba (ed.), *Niewiasty z Pastorałami: Portrety Ksień Klasztoru Benedyktynek Ormiańskich we Lwowie: Historia, Konteksty, Konserwacja*, Kraków, 2022.

118 I would like to express my deepest gratitude to Dr Ara Sayegh for his assistance in preparing this section. See Sayegh, Ara, "Lehahay gawazanakir miandznuhiner" (Polish-Armenian Crosier-Carrying Nuns), *Hayrenikʻ*, 18 May 2023, <https://hairenikweekly.com/?p=56239>, accessed on 15 January 2024.

119 See Zięba, *Niewiasty z Pastorałami*, p. 358; Księgarnia Akademicka Publishing: <https://books.akademicka.pl/publishing/catalog/book/405>.

The first information about the Armenian presence in the Ukrainian and Polish territories is featured in Armenian historiography in the 11th century.[120] The Armenian diaspora of Poland was formed during the 11th–12th centuries on the territories of Galicia, Volhynia, and Podolia which then passed under Polish control in the 14th century. Until the 14th century, the religious centre of the Armenians of Halych, Chełm, Kamieniec Podolski, Volodymyr of Volyn, Lutsk, and Lwów was considered to be Lutsk. In the 1340s, the Polish King Casimir III the Great conquered Galicia and a part of Volhynia. Lutsk, with its St Stepʻanos Armenian church and episcopal centre, remained in the hands of Lithuanian prince Liubartas. To keep the Armenian church safe from the political influence of Lithuanian authorities, in 1367, by a special edict, Casimir the Great granted an official status to the Armenian Diocese and moved it from Lutsk to the royal city of Lwów, where the Armenian community had had a wooden church since 1183 and a brick church since 1251.[121]

In 1356, along with extensive privileges, Casimir the Great granted the Armenian communities of Lwów and Kamieniec Podolski the right to build churches and monasteries. In 1363, the construction of Lwów's stone church of the Dormition of the Holy Mother of God was completed, and in 1367, it became a cathedral church recognised as the centre of the Diocese of the Armenian Apostolic Church in Poland, Moldova, and Romania. In the 16th century, nine Armenian churches and monasteries were functioning in Lwów and its vicinity. Among them, the most prominent were the Cathedral of the Dormition of the Holy Mother of God, St Anna, and St Jacob of Nisibis churches which had a joint monastery, as well as the church of the Holy Cross, which had its own monastery.[122]

---

120 See Vardan Khachʻatryan, "Haykakan gaghtʻavayrerĕ mijnadarum. Lehastan ew Arewmtyan Ukraina" (The Armenian Diaspora in Middle Ages: Poland and Western Ukraine), *Hayotsʻ Patmutʻiwn* (History of Armenia), Vol. II, Book II (second half of the 9th c. – first half of the 17th c.), Yerevan, 2014, pp. 698-702; p. 698.

121 See ibid., p. 699; Bella Barseghyan, "Lehahayotsʻ kronakan hamaynkʻ" (The Armenian Religious Community of Poland), *Kʻristonya Hayastan*, Yerevan, 2002, p. 410; Petros Hovhannisyan, "Lehastani haykakan gaghtʻavayrerĕ XVI-XVII darerum (gaghtʻakanutʻyan ughinerĕ, zhamanakĕ, teghabashkhumĕ, tʻvakʻanakĕ, zbaghmukʻĕ)" (The Armenian Settlements in Poland in 16th–17th Centuries [Routes of Emigration, Time, Distribution, Number, Occupation]), *Ējmiatsin* 1, 2009, pp. 63-68.

122 Khachʻatryan, "Haykakan gaghtʻavayrerĕ mijnadarum", pp. 698-699; Barseghyan, "Lehahayotsʻ kronakan hamaynkʻ", p. 410.

Between the 11th and 14th centuries, twelve churches were constructed in Kamieniec Podolski. In 1250, there was a functioning church, which was later destroyed, and in 1394, the Church of St Nicholas, the oldest among the extant churches of the city, was built. A century later, this same church was renamed the Church of the Dormition of the Holy Mother of God. In 1498, a larger and even more glorious church with the same name was built. Then, in 1522, the Church of the Annunciation of the Holy Mother of God was constructed. Besides the 20-22 churches built in the cities of Lutsk, Lwów, and Kamieniec Podolski, in 16th-18th centuries over twenty churches functioned in Armenian diasporic centres in Lublin, Zamość, Kubachivsty, Yaroslav, Tysmenytsya, Yazlovets', Zloczow (Zolochiv), Zhvanets, Sniatyn, Stanyslaviv (Ivano-Frankivsk), Lysets', Berezhany, Mohyliv-Podil'skyi, and Rashkiv.

In 1364, with a special edict, Catholicos Mesrop I Artazets'i (1359-1372) established the Armenian Diocese of Poland, anointing Bishop Grigor as its primate.[123] Before the conversion of the Armenian communities of Poland, which was a result of religious oppression and their inclusion in the Catholic Church, the Diocese of the Armenian Church in Poland followed the authority of the Mother See of Holy Ējmiatsin in matters related to faith.[124]

Naturally, Armenian immigrants brought their national culture, customs, and church traditions from their homeland in order to create a prosperous community, like the one on the Crimean Peninsula, whose existence has been known since the 9th-11th centuries, and to the Armenian colonies formed on the territory of Poland. This included church organizational structures not only composed of men, but also of women.

The first traces of the Armenian nunnery of Lwów date back to the 16th century. In the second half of the 17th century, there was a community with the name of "Virtuous Armenian Women" (*Hayazgi barepasht tiknants' miabanut'iwn*) in the church of the Dormition of the Holy Mother of God of Kamieniec Podolski.[125] It should be noted that in 1600, Archbishop Grigor Varagets'i had a monastery built for the Armenian nuns next to the Church

---

123 See Ezeants', Karapet (trans. and ed.), *Brni miut'iwn Hayots' Lehastani ĕnd Ekeghets'woyn Hṛomay. Zhamanakakits' yishatakarank'* (Forced Union of the Armenians of Poland with the Roman Church: Contemporary Memoires), St Petersburg, 1884, p. xix; Ōrmanean, Maghak'ia, *Azgapatum*, Vol. II, Constantinople, 1914, p. 2175; Barseghyan, "Lehahayots' kronakan hamaynk'", ibid.

124 Ibid.; see also Khach'atryan, "Haykakan gaght'avayrerĕ mijnadarum", pp. 698-702.

125 Zięba, *Niewiasty z Pastorałami*, p. 358.

of the Annunciation of the Holy Mother of God in Kamieniec Podolski.[126] After 1670, Ṛipʻsima (Hṛipʻsimē) Spendowska and two other nuns, Anna Bogdanowiczówna and Anna Mikoyalowa, who joined her, began their monastic life in the city of Jazłowiec. Ṛipʻsima Spendowska, accompanied by her mother, went on a pilgrimage to Jerusalem, where she joined her father, Sefer[127] Astuatsaturowicz[128], who had been in Jerusalem since 1653 in the "service of the Holy Tomb". On the Holy Tomb of Christ in Jerusalem, Ṛipʻsima Spendowska took a special vow, dedicating herself to "eternal celibacy". Following her father's and husband's death in Jerusalem, she returned with her mother to Jazłowiec, where she was consecrated as a nun by Archbishop Nikol Tʻorosowicz in accordance with the Armenian monastic tradition.[129] However, in 1672, the nuns mentioned above, fearful of imminent Turkish invasion, were forced to leave Jazłowiec. Two of them went to Brody, after which, all three of them settled in Lwów with their respective relatives, separating from one another.[130]

Unfortunately, following the Turkish incursions of 1672-1699, the nunnery adjacent to the Church of the Annunciation of the Holy Mother of God in Kamieniec Podolski, along with the church itself, was destroyed. Initially, the Armenian nuns remained hidden but later were forced to abandon the city with the rest of the Armenians, fleeing via the Black Sea to Filibe (now Plovdiv, Bulgaria). From there, they returned to Stanyslaviv through the territories of the Danubian Principalities several years later, after which they settled in Lwów.[131] This must have happened at the end of 1675 and the start of 1676.[132] This event ultimately had a positive outcome for all the Armenian nuns who found refuge in Lwów, for instead of living separately with their relatives, they created a monastic community. Early on, three of the nuns from Jazłowiec and fourteen from Kamieniec Podolski joined together, calling their newly founded community the *Surb Hṛipʻsimeantsʻ Kusanatsʻ Miabanutʻiwn* (Nunnery of St Hṛipʻsimian Virgins).[133] Soon after, the elders of the Armenian

---

126 Sayegh, "Lehahay gawazanakir miandznuhiner".

127 Most likely, his name was Stepʻan (see Zięba, *Niewiasty z Pastorałami*, p. 13).

128 After receiving the title of nobility, the entire family adopts the surname Spendowski.

129 See Zięba, *Niewiasty z Pastorałami*, p. 13.

130 Ibid.

131 Ibid., p. 122; Sayegh, "Lehahay gawazanakir miandznuhiner".

132 Ibid.

133 See Zięba, *Niewiasty z Pastorałami*, p. 13.

community of Lwów provided two houses located near the Armenian cemetery in the northern part of the cathedral, which the nuns turned into a monastery.[134]

It should also be mentioned that before moving to Lwów, the Armenian
nuns had followed a specific monastic order, which may have been based on
the canons traditionally attributed to St Basil of Caesarea. In Lwów, however,
the newly founded monastery of "St Hṛip'simian Virgins" adopted the Benedictine order, which will be discussed below.

The Armenian nuns were commonly referred to as "the virgins" or as
ghĕzlar, a Kipchak word predominantly used in conversations among the Armenians of Poland. They were also referred to as "dewotki", the old Polish
generic term meaning "devoted".[135]

Despite the fact that the three Armenian monasteries of Kamieniec Podolski, Jazłowiec, and Lwów were founded on European soil, the nuns, main-
taining a degree of isolation from secular life in their daily routines, preserved
the centuries-long tradition of Armenian monasticism. They studied the Holy
Scriptures, observed the canonical hours, prayed, and provided pastoral care,
especially to girls and women, when they were in need of spiritual and moral
support. There is also evidence that they offered their services during the baptism of girls, especially young ladies.[136]

The most interesting material relevant to our study is the evidence pertaining to the existence of ordained deaconesses among these nuns. Even
though the authors of the book *Niewiasty z Pastorałami* (Women with Crosiers) mentioned just two deaconesses,[137] it should be noted that to begin with,
there were other deaconesses within these three monasteries who conducted
specific ceremonial services within the enclosed environment of the nunnery,
including the canonical hours that involved sections with the participation of
deacons, ceremonial readings of the Holy Gospel, and so on. Only deaconesses were permitted to perform them as deacons were not allowed to enter
the restricted areas of the nunnery.

Unfortunately, there is little relevant information about one of the deaconesses mentioned in the book. The aforementioned nun Ṛip'sima
(Hṛip'simē) Spendowska from Jazłowiec is mentioned, with Roberta R. Ervin

---

134 Ibid., p. 49; Pronislawa K'ēōp'riwlean Vuicic, "Lehastani hay patmakan yisha-
       takaranneru ts'uts'ahandēsĕ" (The Exhibition of Armenian Historical Artifacts
       of Poland), *Anahit* 3-6, 1932-1933, pp. 38-53; p. 47.
135 Sayegh, "Lehahay gawazanakir miandznuhiner".
136 Ibid.
137 Zięba, *Niewiasty z Pastorałami*, p. 385.

writing that she travelled to Jerusalem on a pilgrimage with her parents and, upon her return to Jazłowiec, she was ordained a deaconess.[138] However, the biography of Ṙip'sima Spendowska in Niewiasty z Pastorałami does not include these details,[139] and the esteemed author does not provide any documentary sources for this material in their work.[140]

The information about the second Armenian deaconess from Kamieniec Podolski, Mariana (Maria) Poghosowna (Maryanna Bohosówna) (1630-1690), is worthy of special attention. She was the daughter of Pōghos and Horpina Poghosowicz, well-respected members of the local Armenian community. They were related to Bogdan Seferowicz Spendowski, who married Gulaf Zadigowiczówna in Kamieniec and who was the brother of Hṙip'simē Spendowska. The latter was one of the founders of the St Hṙip'simian Virgins nunnery.[141]

Mariana's sister, Ustiana, was married to a Polish-Armenian named Shimka from Kamieniec, while her brother, Yakob Poghosowicz (d. 1695), held a prominent position in the Armenian community of Kamieniec Podolski.[142]

Most likely in 1652, Mariana travelled to Jerusalem on a pilgrimage and, on her way, passed through Constantinople. Before that, disagreements had arisen between the Catholicosate of All Armenians and the Sis Catholicosate regarding the jurisdiction of the Sees of the Catholicoi and the ordination of bishops for dioceses, which was exacerbated during the patriarchate of P'ilippos I Aghbakets'i (1633-1655) and Catholicos of Sis, Simeon II Sebastats'i

---

138 See R. Roberta Ervine, "The Armenian Church's Women Deacons", *St. Nersess Theological Review* 12, 2007, pp. 17-56; pp. 18, 38. See also O. Knarik Meneshian, "A Nearly Forgotten History: Women Deacons in the Armenian Church", *The Armenian weekly*", 6 July 2013, <https://armenianweekly.com/2013/07/06/a-nearly-forgotten-history-women-deacons-in-the-armenian-church/> (accessed on 16 January 2024): "In Jazlowiec (pronounced Yaswovietch), Hripsime Spendowski was ordained a deaconess. She was the daughter of Stepan Spendowski, an Armenian who had immigrated to Jazlowiec in 1648. The town had a sizeable Armenian population, and the Armenian Prelacy was established there in 1250. Because of Spendowski's heroism and distinguished military service fighting the Tatars and Turks who had invaded the town, the King of Poland honored him with the rank of nobility, and bestowed upon him the title of 'mayor for life' of Jazlowiez."

139 Zięba, *Niewiasty z Pastorałami*, p. 122.

140 See Ervine, "The Armenian Church's Women Deacons", p. 38.

141 Zięba, *Niewiasty z Pastorałami*, p. 207.

142 Ibid.

(1633-1648). Then, during the tenure of the Catholicos of Sis Nersēs V Sebastats'i (1648-1654), an environment of mutual understanding and collaboration emerged between the Catholicosates of Holy Ējmiatsin and Cilicia, which was expressed through the convocation of a church synod.[143]

Marianna Ksawera Nersesowiczówna – the first abbess of the Armenian Benedictine convent from 1701. 18th / 1st half of the 19th century, painter unknown, oil, canvas (photo: Konrad K. Pollesch, Foundation for the Culture and Heritage of Polish Armenians in Warsaw)[144].

---

143 See Ōrmanean, *Azgapatum*, Vol. II, pp. 2444-2464.
144 See Zięba, *Niewiasty z Pastorałami*, p. 16.

Catholicos P'ilippos visited Aleppo via the Karin road, where the See of Sis was located at the time. Then, on the occasion of the feast of Easter, both catholicoi travelled to Jerusalem on a pilgrimage and participated in the church synod.[145] After settling the disagreements between the Mother See and the Cilician Catholicosate, in 1653, on his way to Ējmiatsin, Catholicos P'ilippos travelled by sea to Constantinople to address the issues surrounding the Armenian patriarchate of Constantinople.[146] It was at this particular time that a group of Armenians from Poland, including the catholic Archbishop Nikol T'orosowicz, arrived in Constantinople to seek a solution, with the help of the authority of the Catholicos, for the issues that had arisen in the Armenian community of Poland.[147] History does not provide us with accurate information on whether Mariana Poghosowna's visit to Constantinople and her meeting with Catholicos P'ilippos I Aghbakets'i had any connection with the visit of the Armenians of Poland or of Nikol T'orosowicz.[148] Nevertheless, she was there during the negotiations, and it is a fact that in 1653, she was ordained a deaconess personally by Catholicos P'ilippos I Aghbakets'i. Regrettably, Armenian historiographical sources do not offer any information regarding the conditions and reasons for this ordination. However, most significant aspect of this event for us is that Catholicos P'ilippos I Aghbakets'i, being one of the custodians of the law and order of the Armenian Church and a dedicated guardian of its traditions, would not have performed such an ordination without being convinced that this clerical order and tradition existed in the Armenian Church.

---

145 Ibid. Editors, "Kat'oghikos" (Catholicos), *K'ristonya Hayastan*, Yerevan, 2002, pp. 457-470; p. 464.

146 For this sequence of events, see Aṛak'el Dawrizhest'i, *Patmut'iwn*, p. 334; Ezeants', *Bṛni miut'iwn Hayots' Lehastani ěnd Ekeghets'woyn Hṛomay*, p. xxix; Ōrmanean, *Azgapatum*, vol. II, pp. 2476-2481.

147 Ibid.

148 There is very scant and often contradictory biographic information about Mariana Poghosowna. According to the details supplied by the Dominican friar Sadok Barącz (1814-1892) in his *Żywoty sławnych Ormian w Polsce* (Lives of famous Armenians in Poland) (Lwów, 1856, pp. 98-99), Mariana Poghosowna lived in Kamieniec Podolski with her fellow nuns and in 1650 she went on a pilgrimage to Jerusalem. On the way there, she visited Ējmiatsin, from where she went to Constantinople, where she was ordained a deaconess by Catholicos P'ilippos I Aghbakets'i. It is not clear whether she accompanied the Catholicos from Ējmiatsin to Jerusalem and then from Jerusalem to Constantinople. See also Zięba, *Niewiasty z Pastorałami*, p. 207.

From the Polish sources and the testimonies of Armenian nuns who were her contemporaries we find out that, after her ordination, deaconess Mariana Poghosowna travelled to Rome to worship the relics of the Lord's apostles. From there, she returned to Kamieniec Podolski to his sisters, the nuns. According to their testimonies, after she had received a monastic rank in Rome, Mariana began to wear a short black shawl, a cowl-like cover on her head, a belt over her waist, and travel shoes on her feet, like the Bernardine nuns. She was proud that the Catholicos had ordained her as deaconess, and as a result of her position, she would read the Holy Gospel and the *Life of Saints* to the nuns who did not have the relevant authority to do so. She also tried to persuade the other nuns to wear the Bernardine nuns' habit and to elect her as the monastery's abbess. However, since the nuns refused to wear the Bernardine habits and to elect her as the abbess, Mariana Poghosowna left Kamieniec Podolski and went to Stanyslaviv, where her brother, Yakob Poghosowicz, lived.[149]

Unfortunately, historians do not supply any further noteworthy details about Mariana Poghosowna's activities in church matters. Did she manage to fulfil her full duties as a deaconess in accordance with her office in the Armenian communities or one of the nunneries in Stanyslaviv? We do not know. Irrespective of that, a valuable historical fact remains, which is that with Mariana Pogosowna's ordination, the tradition of deaconesses in the Armenian Church continued to be preserved, reaching the remote Armenian communities in the diaspora.

The forcible conversion of the Armenian communities of Poland to Catholicism in the 17th century was an unfortunate expression of the uncompromising confessional policies led by Archbishop Nikol T'orosowicz and Rome. The Armenian nuns, who had assembled in Lwów, were not, of course, spared the tempest of religious confrontations that struck the Armenian communities of Poland. To preserve their existence and successfully pursue their introspective life devoted to prayers, they agreed to adopt Catholicism. In June 1688, the abbess of the catholic nunnery of Lwów, Eleonora Kazanowska, appealed to Rome on behalf of the Armenian nuns to establish a new monastery for them.[150] The successor of Nikol T'orosowicz, Archbishop Vardan Yunanean (1644-1715), also sent a separate epistle to Rome regarding this matter.[151]

---

149 Zięba, *Niewiasty z Pastorałami*, pp. 122, 207; Barącz, *Żywoty sławnych Ormian w Polsce*, pp. 98-99.
150 Zięba, *Niewiasty z Pastorałami*, p. 51.
151 Ibid.

In 1690, Pope Alexander IX approved the new nunnery for the Armenian nuns, allowing them to preserve the Armenian rite but ensuring that they adopted the religious order of St Benedict. On November 26, 1691, a ceremony of the blessing of the 15 newly consecrated nuns took place at the Cathedral of the Dormition of the Holy Mother of God in Lwów.[152] A year later, in 1692, upon completing the novitiate, they took their vows of continence with the blessing of Archbishop Vardan Yunanean.[153] It should be mentioned that Nikol Tʿorosowicz had previously consecrated nine of these nuns, and by the time this group of Armenian nuns had agreed to adopt the religious order of St Benedict and were newly consecrated, their number had increased by six.[154]

In 1701, the Armenian nuns of this newly founded convent elected a new abbess, Marianna Nersesoviczowna, who had earlier been in a catholic Benedictine nunnery of Yaroslav. She was the first to receive the bishop's crosier, ring, and the right to wear the pectoral cross.[155] No matter how privileged this phenomenon was within the Armenian monastic environment in Poland at this time, we are well aware of abbesses who had the same privileges: the pastoral stick, pectoral cross, and the right to wear a ring in the Armenian tradition.[156] In addition the episcopal crosier[157] is the symbol of the pastoral office

---

152 The names of the 15 nuns are: Rypsyma Benedykta Spendowska, Helena Gertruda Jalinówna, Anna Mechtylda Milkiewiczówna (Miłkiewiczówna), Zuzanna Ludgarda Milkiewiczówna (Miłkiewiczówna), Anna Maura Emirowiczówna, Anna Febronia Milkiewiczówna (Miłkiewiczówna), Katarzyna Columbus Balicka, Marianna Serafina Bernatowiczówna, Anna Beata Bernatowiczówna, Helena Fortunata Spendowska, Zofia Apollinara Baltazarowiczówna, Marianna Romualda Bogdanówna and Helena Aniela Piramowiczówna (ibid.).

153 Ibid.

154 Ibid.

155 Ten other abbesses, who also received the bishop's crosier, ring, and the right to wear the pectoral cross, succeeded Marianna Nersesoviczowna (see ibid., p. 376).

156 Evidence of this is provided by photos of other Armenian nunneries in which the abbesses are at least holding a staff in their hand, wearing a pectoral cross and a ring on their finger.

157 The episcopal or pastoral crosier was introduced in the Armenian Church similar to the crosier of the Catholic Church. In its upper part, there is a rounded head that is turned inwards. It also features bud-like ornaments resembling the blossoming staff of Aaron, the High Priest. Episcopal crosiers resemble ordinary pastoral crosiers, which is why they are also called pastoral crosiers. At the end of the rotating part of these crosiers, there is also a snake's head (only one snake). See *Araratean Hayrapetakan Tʿem, Zoravor Surb Astvatsatsin Ekeghetsʿi, "Gavazan"*

of the church, the Armenian Church also has a *vardapet*'s crosier[158], which is the symbol of the true doctrine.

This was not a completely new innovation for the Roman Catholic Church either, as this tradition already existed in some female monastic orders. In fact, it was customary for the abbesses of Benedictine and Cistercian monasteries to carry a "matriarchal crosier", which is precisely the same as an episcopal crosier. Like bishops, they also usually wore a ring and a pectoral cross. Throughout history, these abbesses were authorised to read from the Holy Gospel during solemn ceremonies. Similar to bishops, they often had jurisdiction not only in the convent but also in the surrounding communities.[159]

After the Second World War, the Armenian Benedictine nuns of Lwów left their original nunnery located near the Cathedral of the Dormition of the Holy Mother of God and established in the Benedictine nunnery in Lublin, where the last abbess, Elekta Orlowska, died in 1954. The remaining nuns then moved to Wołów in 1954-1958. There, in 1961, that Armenian congregation of nuns joined the Latin Benedictine order and subsequently, completely renounced the Armenian rite.

(Crosier), published online on 29 April 2015, <https://surbzoravor.am/post/view/gavazan≥, accessed 18 January 2024.

158 The crosiers of *vardapet*s are serpent-headed. Two-, four-, or more-headed serpents symbolise the true doctrine by which salvation is attained. It is made in the likeness of the snake of Moses, which saved those who looked at it in the desert. In the head part of the double-headed staff, the heads of the snakes face each other; in the middle, there is an orb, which symbolises the world with a cross on top; the lower parts of the snakes are connected to each other. The four-headed crosiers have no ritual difference from the two-headed crosiers: they are simply more decorative. During the rapprochement with the Latin Church, Catholicos Grigor IV Tghay received a full priestly dress from Pope Lucius III in 1184, after which the use of snake-headed crosiers passed to the *vardapet*s (ibid.).

159 See Gerlinde von Westphalen, *Lady Abess. Benedicta von Spiegel Politische Ordensfrau in der NS-Zeit*, 2nd ed., Münster, 2023; Katholische Kirche, Bistum Limburg, "Ring und Stab für die Hirtin der Abtei: Sr. Katharina Drouvé hat von Bischof Bätzing die Äbtissinnenweihe empfangen", published online on 5 March 2023, <https://bistumlimburg.de/beitrag/ring-und-stab-fuer-die-hirtin-der-abtei-1/>, accessed 18 January 2024.

St Katarinē's Convent of New Julfa

Following testimonies about deaconesses from Cilician and Eastern Armenia in earlier centuries, in the 17th century we encounter deaconesses in organised monastic centres beyond the borders of Armenia again, specifically in the convent of St Katarinē (Catharine) in New Julfa in what is now known as Iran. The convent was built in the year 1072 of the Armenian Era (= 1623) through the efforts of *xoja* Eghiazar. The first nuns who resided there were the virgins Uṛukʿsana, Tʿaguhi, and Hṛipʿsimē, who had found refuge near the church of St Yovhannēs of New Julfa after their forced migration organised by Shah Abbas (Abbas the Great, 1571-1629). They brought the relics of St Katarinē (to whom the women's convent was dedicated), St Hṛipʿsimē, and St John the Baptist from Armenia. The convent, also referred to as a "hermitage", was surrounded by tall protective walls and around the centrally located church were the nuns' cells.

In the first 50 years of its existence, the number of nuns increased to 33, but this figure gradually decreased thereafter. A later attempt to revive the number of the convent's members in 1937 failed, and it was closed in 1954 after becoming devoid of inhabitants. The convent also had a school for girls. After taking monastic vows, a step undertaken after reaching the age of 20, novices received the four minor clerical ranks from the bishop.

With regard to the tradition of ordination of deaconesses in the hermitage of St Katarinē, we should mention that this initiative was mistakenly attributed to Tʿadēos Peknazarean, the diocesan bishop of the Armenians of Persia and India (1851-1863)[160]. However, evidence suggests the existence of deaconesses in the convent before 1660, for in the colophon of the *Khorhrdatetr* (Missal 1641-1660) copied by the priest Yakob, there is a mention of the names of more than a dozen deaconesses of St Katarinē's Convent:

> Glory [...] The life-giving mystery of the Divine Liturgy was completed by my, the unworthy priest Yakob's hand, in the city of Ĕspahan (Isfahan), in the village called Jughay (Julfa), at the door of the holy virgin Katarinē, in the year 1109 of the Armenian Era (= 1660) [...]

---

160 See Ter-Yakobjaneantsʿ, H., *Tʿadēos Arkepiskwposi Peknazarean Arajnord Hayotsʿ Parskastani ew Hndkastani 1851-1863*, Biography of the Archbishop Tʿadēos Peknazarean, diocesan bishop of the Armenians of Persia and India 1851-1863, *Ararat*, 1906, pp. 351-362 <https://arar.sci.am/dlibra/publication/86126/edition/77895/content>, accessed 3 April 2024.

May you also remember the nuns of the holy congregation and the neophytes who have assembled here: the deaconesses Saṛa and Trisiē, Sandukht and the younger Saṛa, Gayianē, Hughitē, Marinos, T'aguhi, Hṛip'simē, Eghisabet', Dshkho, Varvaṛ; the *mahdasi*[161] virgins – the other Ughitē, the abbess T'an-kik, Maram, Ana, Ishkhan, Nuni, and the other Ana; also the servants of the church – Hṛup'sanē, Shushan, Mart'ē, Eprak'sē, Sup'iē, the other Varvaṛ, Na-najan, the other T'aguhi, the other Hṛip'simē, T'alit'ē, the gatekeeper Marga-rit, the hardworking Pōghos, and the convent's deceased nuns [...]

May you remember the servants of this holy church – T'ekghiē, Eghinar, Maram, Mamar, may you remember ...[162]

It is possible that the tradition of ordaining deaconesses at St Katarinē's Convent was halted some time before 1660 for a period, and, considering the established precedent within the convent, Archbishop T'adēos Peknazarean then reinstated it in 1851 with his episcopal and authoritative status.[163]

---

161 See above, note 91.

162 Hakobyan, Vazgen (ed.), *Hayeren dzeṛagreri ZhĒ dari hishatakaranner (1641-1660)* (The Colophons of Armenian Manuscripts of the 17th Century [1641-1660]), Vol. III, Yerevan, 1984, pp. 960-961: Փառք ...: Աղաչեցաք կենսատու խորհուրդդ սուրբ պատարագիս ձեռամբ անարժան Յակոբ քահանայիս, ի քաղաքս Ըսպահան, ի գեօղն որ կոչի Չուղայ, ի դուռն սուրբ կուսիս Կատարինեա, ի թվականութեանս Հայոց ՌՃԹ (1660) ...

Դարձեալ յիշեցէք զմիաբան սուրբ ուխտիս, որ են ժողովեալ աստ զարքբասանեալ կուսանքս, եւ որ ի սմա են եկամուտ, զսարկաւագուհիքն՝ զՍառէն եւ Տրիսիէն, զՄանդուխտն եւ փոքր Սառէն, զԳայիանէն, Յուղիտէն, Մարինոսն, Թագուհին, Հռիփսիմէն, Եղիսաբեթն, Դշխոյին, Վարվառն: Զմահդասիքն՝ միւս Ուղիտէն, զմայրապետ Թանկիկն, Մարամն եւ Աննային, Իշխանն, զՆունին եւ միւս Անային: Եւ սպասաւորք եկեղեցւոյն՝ Հռուփսանէն, Շուշանն, Մարթէն, Եպրաքսէն, Սուփիէն, զմիւս Վարվառն, զնանաջանն, միւս Թագուհին, միւս Հռիփսիմէն, Թալիթէն, դռնապան Մարգրիտն, բազմաշխատ Պողոսն, եւ հանգուցեալ միաբանք սողին ...

Յիշեցէք սուրբ եկեղեցւոյս զսպասաւոր Թեկղիէն, Եղինարն, Մարամն, Մամարն, յիշեցէք ... According to Father Khorēn Khuts'ean and the information conveyed by Ter-Hovhannisyants', Archbishop T'adēos Peknazarean, being impressed by the women's convent of St Step'anos in Tbilisi and its consecrated nuns, introduced the tradition of deaconesses into his diocese in 1851 by performing ordinations in St Katarinē's Convent (see Khuts'ean, Khorēn, *T'iflisi S. Step'anos kusanats' anapati patmut'iwnĕ* [The History of St Step'anos's Convent of Tiflis], Tbilisi, 1914, p. 95).

163 See Mkrtch'yan, "Sarkavaguhineri tsaṛayut'yunn u pashtonĕ Hay Aṛak'elakan Ekeghets'um", p. 47.

Only a few of the virgins might have been ordained as deaconesses to preach the Gospel and fulfil certain religious functions, while the remaining large number of them received the four minor clerical ranks.

In 1933, an interesting document regarding the convent of St Katarinē of New Julfa appeared in the pages of the monthly periodical *Hay Khōsnak* (Armenian Speaker), published in Constantinople. At the time, it was passed on by Arshak Alpōyachean to Abbess Aghawni K'ēōsēean during his visit to Cairo. It will not be superfluous to quote this document, as it offers a glimpse into the convent mentioned above:

> As can be observed, there is an image of a dwelling place in the New Julfa convent at the top of the document: "built [in] the sacred hermitage of holy, luminous virgin Katarinē." Surrounding it are images of sixteen nuns wearing mantle-like robes, all confessing within the same convent. The veil of their superior is shaped like a cowl, and their faces are covered up to their mouths. Their names are visible beneath each image. On the top left side, the first image is that of the abbess, who is holding the abbess's crosier.

> The document's content is a request "from the resplendent, honest, and courageous commander-in-chief, Koṙnel [Koronel?] Agha Yakob Petrosean, who is adorned with God's grace" [...] "in support of the assiduously praying virgins who inhabit the convent's cells." The text is signed by "the confessors and the praying members of this holy hermitage – Abbess Katarinē, Eghisabet', Vaṙvaṙ, and ordinary virgins." The text bears the date 1839, "month of May," etc., from which we may infer that it is 94 years old, and, undoubtedly, "New Julfa's wonderful holy hermitage of the all-knowing, holy virgin Katarinē" had an ecclesiastical spiritual organisation including virgins with church titles, up to the rank of archdeaconess.[164]

In this document, Katarinē, the abbess of the nunnery, is of utmost significance, for she was not only an ordained archdeaconess: she held the abbess's crosier in her right hand. Much like the *vardapet*'s crosier, symbolizing the authority to teach the doctrine of the Armenian Church, we observe that the abbess of this nunnery also carries a crosier, granting her the authority to lead the nunnery and provide spiritual education to the nuns accordingly.

Regarding the 16 images of nuns featured in the document mentioned above, it is worth noting that in the periodical *Bazmavēp* from 1989, a translation of an interesting text titled "Niwt'er hay vanakanut'ean patmut'ean"

---

164 See Alpōyachean, Arshak *Hay Khōsnak* (Armenian Speaker), IX, 5-6, 1933, pp. 80-81.

(Sources for the History of Armenian Monasticism) was published.[165] This work was also published in a separate *Bazmavēp* volume, in which there is a photograph of five virgins from St Katarinē's Convent of New Julfa. Their vestments correspond fully to those seen in the images of the 16 nuns inserted in the margins of Alpōyachean's document. The novice virgin standing on the right side of the photograph, dressed in a mantle with a headcover shaped like a cowl, merits attention. It is plausible that this historical testimony was prepared for her ordination.

Father Khorēn Khuts'ean has addressed the history of St Katarinē's Convent of New Julfa while discussing the history of Tbilisi's St Step'anos's Convent.[166] Within this, he presented the monastic constitution of the former,[167] enabling us to form a broader understanding of both its internal order and the austere monastic life.

The Canons of St Katarinē's Convent of New Julfa

1. St Katarinē's Convent is under the immediate jurisdiction of the spiritual authority of the Diocese.
2. The convent is governed by a governing body called "The Chapter of St Katarinē's Convent", which should consist of experienced priests appointed by the head of the Diocese or the vicar.
3. The governing body of the convent should meet at the convent every Saturday with the aim of improving its social and economic life.
4. One governing body member is appointed treasurer by the spiritual authority of the Diocese. The prelate's office should provide him with a book bound with a ribbon, which will be used to register, in an orderly fashion, the revenues and expenses of the convent.

---

165 See Dadjad Yardemian (trans.), "Niwt'er hay vanakanut'ean patmut'ean" (Sources for the History of Armenian Monasticism), *Bazmavēp* 1-4, 1988, pp. 212-227 and Dadjad Yardemian (trans.), "Niwt'er hay vanakanut'ean patmut'ean" (Sources for the History of Armenian Monasticism), *Bazmavēp* 1-4, 1989, pp. 159-164.

166 Khuts'ean, *T'iflisi S. Step'anos kusanats' anapati patmut'iwnĕ*, pp. 79-100. See also Kiwregh Israyēlean, "Nor-Jughayi S. Katarinēan Anapatĕ" (St Katarinē's Hermitage of New Julfa), *Sion*, 10-12, 1944, pp. 192-199, and ibid., 1, 1945, pp. 23-27. Ēlisabet' T'ajiryan's article on the donation book of St Katarinē's Convent is also highly informative in this respect. See Ēlisabet' T'ajiryan, "Nor Jughayi S. Katarinēants' Kusanats' Vank'i Ĕntsayamateanĕ" (The Donation Book of the St Katarinē's Convent of New Julfa), *Handēs Amsōreay* 1-12, 2023, pp. 133-162.

167 Khuts'ean, *T'iflisi S. Step'anos kusanats' anapati patmut'iwnĕ*, pp. 96-99.

5. The governing body of the convent is responsible for overseeing the estate, revenues, and expenses of the convent. They must never sell or pawn the estate; however, after informing the public on behalf of the prelate's office, they can rent it out.

6. The governing body of the convent may lend money or borrow from others after obtaining permission from the head of the Diocese, the vicar, or the prelate's office.

7. By the order of the head of the diocese, two of the nuns are appointed to the office of expense manager. They are obliged to act with the knowledge and consent of the governing body of the convent and the abbess.

8. Every Saturday, the expense managers must provide the members of the governing body of the convent with detailed accounts of expenditures in the presence of the abbess and all the nuns.

9. At the beginning of each month, the governing body of the convent must review and approve the expenditures and income from the previous month.

10. At the beginning of each year, the same governing body must present all the accounting books, contracts, and lists of last year's rents and expenses for examination and publication before the tribunal of the leadership of the diocese.

11. The nuns and novices must obey the convent's orders and rules strictly. No one is allowed to leave the convent and visit relatives or acquaintances without the abbess's permission.

12. Everyone must be present in the church in an orderly manner for the prayer services.

13. Everyone must obey the convent's governing body and the abbess's orders and directives.

14. The convent's abbess must carefully monitor the morals and habits of the nuns and novices and ensure the orderly performance of the divine service. She must give advice and reprimand those who disobey. If they fail to correct their behaviour after the second admonition, the abbess must inform the governing body of the convent about it. If they do not learn their lesson after being warned and reprimanded again, the governing body of the convent must report all the transgressions of a nun and novice to the head of the Diocese. The head of the Diocese decides the type of punishment, which can include church confessions (for the nuns and novices), a temporary ban on wearing the stole, or banishment from the convent (for the nuns and novices).

15. The nuns must work to support the activities of the New Julfa charity of Armenian women, for it caters to the needs and necessities of orphans and underprivileged female students, providing support for their education and upbringing in the National Institute of Young Ladies.

Ḥṛip'simē Aghek'-T'ahireants', abbess, princess, archdeaconess.

St Step'anos's Convent of Tbilisi

Besides the convent of St Katarinē, we know of three other nunneries where the tradition of the ordination of deaconesses was upheld. The first is St Step'anos's Convent, founded in Tbilisi, which followed the example of St Katarinē convent a hundred years after the latter's establishment. Cognisant of the existence of New Julfa's St. Katarinē's Convent, Prince Ashkharbēg Behbut'eants desired to establish a comparable institution in Tbilisi. However, his dream, ultimately unfulfilled in his lifetime, was accomplished by his son Melik'-Aghabēk Behbut'eants in around 1724-1727 in Tbilisi on the grounds of their family estate.[168] St Step'anos's Convent was under the direct influence of this family for an extended period, to the extent that the abbess was appointed exclusively by this family.

The convent's abbess always held the title of archdeaconess, and the first abbess of the convent was sister T'aguhi, who spent most of her abbacy between 1790 and 1799 in Kizlyar (Dagestan).[169] She was succeeded by Sister Katarinē Amatuni until 1806. Unfortunately, Father Khorēn Khuts'ean, the historian of St Step'anos's Convent, does not speak highly of her leadership.[170] However, a significant contribution to the improvement of the deteriorated conditions of the convent was made by her successor, Sister Yustianē Astuatsatreants' (1806-1839), whose abbacy was confirmed by Catholicos *Dawit' Bayazetts'i*[171]. In this period, around twenty of the nuns of St Step'anos's Convent were in Kizlyar. After a request from the nuns of the convent, Archbishop Yovsēp' Erkaynabazuk (Long-armed) Arghut'eants', who was recognised as the Catholicos of all Armenians by the decree of Tsar Pavel on 28 July 1800, through the Catholicos's decree, appointed Nun Mariam, probably from the

---

168 The author of the history of the convent, Father Khorēn, writes that during the service of the Holy Liturgy, the virgins in the "Thanksgiving" section utter the following commemoration: "And also for the builders of this holy church: the late Melik'-Ashkharbēk and Mariam, and his sons Behbut' and Minishkar Agha, who are laid to rest under its protection" (see Khuts'ean "T'iflisi S. Step'anos kusanats' anapati patmut'iwnē", pp. 16-17).

169 Ibid., pp. 23-24.

170 Ibid., pp. 27-28.

171 The list of the catholicoi of all Armenians does not include the name of Dawit' Bayazetts'i. Does the author confuse him with Catholicos Dawit' V Ēnēgēt'ts'i (Ghorghanean), the Catholicos of all Armenians in 1801-1807? Sister Yustianē Astuatsatreants' was confirmed in the role of the abbess of the nunnery one year before the death of the Catholicos.

Behbut'ean clan, as the abbess of the convent in Kizlyar.[172] As we know, on his way to Ējmiatsin, Yovsēp' Arghut'eants' fell ill and died in Tbilisi without receiving the unction of the Catholicos. He is not, therefore, listed in the official chronological table of the Armenian Catholicoi. As a result, the congregation of St Step'anos's Convent acquired two abbesses simultaneously – one abbess in Kizlyar and another in Tbilisi, both confirmed in their position through the Catholicos's decree. When Abbess Mariam moved from Kizlyar to Tbilisi with the nuns of her congregation, a confrontation arose between the two abbesses holding the same position. It lasted for some time, however, due to her age, Sister Mariam passed away earlier than Sister Yustianē, who died in 1839.[173] Sister Yustianē was then succeeded by Sister Gayianē Behbut'eants', the abbess whose grandfather was the founder of St Step'anos's Convent of Tbilisi. This abbess truly brought prosperity to St Step'anos's Convent through numerous construction activities and passed away at an advanced age in 1875.[174] She was succeeded by Hrip'simē Begdabēkeants', whose abbacy was short-lived.[175] Between 1877-1898 the abbess was Sister Katarinē Arghut'eats', who was ordained in Sanahin in 1836 but had been a member of the nunnery's congregation for a long time.[176] She was the niece of the earlier mentioned Archbishop Yovsēp' Arghut'eants'. After her, it was Sister P'ep'ronia Khbeants'[177] and then Yep'rosinē Abamelik'ean until 1911.[178] The last abbess of St Step'anos's Convent of Tbilisi was the archdeaconess princess Hrip'simē Aghek'-T'ahireants',who was an influential and highly esteemed individual. She died in 1934 and was buried in Ējmiatsin in the monastic cemetery next to the church of St Gayianē.[179]

As mentioned above, the convent's abbess held the title of the archdeaconess, and wore one or two pectoral crosses, and a ring on the ring finger.

Among the primary responsibilities of deaconesses was visiting the homes of the deceased and consoling those who grieved. Furthermore, at the

---

172 Khuts'ean, *T'iflisi S. Step'anos kusanats' anapati patmut'iwně*, p. 48.
173 Ibid., p. 51.
174 Ibid., pp. 51, 57.
175 Ibid., p. 65.
176 Ibid., pp. 65-66.
177 Ibid., p. 68.
178 Ibid., pp. 69-70.
179 See Henrik Khaṛatean, "T'iblisi S. Step'anos kusanats' anapati ew mayrapet ishkhanuhi Hrip'simē T'ahireants'i masin (About St Step'anos's Convent and Hrip'simē T'ahireants', the Abbess Princess)", *Ejmiatsin* 5, 2007, pp. 87-91; p. 89.

abbess's command, some nuns sang songs of lament over the deceased, invited grieving women to the church, and sang *sharakan*s and psalms during the memorial services.

An eyewitness account of St Step'anos's Convent of Tbilisi was provided by Melik' Bēylik'chean, and appeared in 1895 in the newspaper *Hayrenik' Ōragir* (Gazette Fatherland) printed in Constantinople; the same content was reprinted in the *Hay Khōsnak* (The Armenian Speaker) in 1933.[180] To form a more complete picture of the life and daily routine of the convent, we deem it appropriate to present a condensed overview below:

> After visiting all the great public establishments of this large Caucasian capital, I was naturally intrigued to see the Armenian convent and the chapel of St Step'anos, whose pointed dome always caught my eye while passing through the wide avenues.
>
> On Sunday, 20 October [1895], led by an acquaintance of mine, I visited the chapel to attend a memorial service which was conducted by the nuns. Their heads and faces were almost completely covered with black veils, with delicate white needlework threads extending over them to their feet. Each of them was wearing a *dpir*'s robe of a specific colour, secured with a gold-embroidered belt. Some were holding candles in their hands, while two were swinging the thurible. As always, during this divine ceremony, the only male present was the priest celebrating the liturgy, for *there were nuns who had reached the rank of protodeacon and could not celebrate the liturgy alone.* When invited, they also participate in funerals in the capacity of *dpir*s and deacons.
>
> In this divine, holy place, the nuns' gentle and accomplished singing, especially of the mournful melodies of memorial services, evokes an unusual sense of awe and sorrow in individuals, more so when you observe that these elderly nuns are also profoundly moved, wishing to conceal their tears, as indicated by the movements of their handkerchiefs. Everything here inspires holiness and faith, and you feel yourself in the house of God.
>
> Then, the nun Manya Loris-Melik'yan invites us into her cell, devoid of decorations but equipped with everything necessary for a peaceful, quiet, and

---

180 Mkrtchyan, "Sarkavaguhineri tsaṛayut'yunn u pashtoně Hay aṛak'elakan ekeghets'um", p. 45; see also Bēylik'chean, Melik', "Awag sarkawaguhiner hay kusastanneri mej" (Archdeaconesses in Armenian Nunneries), *Hayrenik' Ōragir*, 26 November 1895, p. 2 and Bēylik'chean, Melik', "Awag sarkawaguhiner hay kusastanneri mej" (Archdeaconesses in Armenian Nunneries), *Hay Khōsnak*, IX, 5-6, 1933, pp. 79-82.

simple life. After a brief visit, we introduce ourselves to Mother Superior, duchess Katarinē Erkaynabazuk Arghut'eants' the Abbess – an old, short, and chubby woman, covered in black from head to toe, sitting in the corner of an oriental sofa in a tidy, middle-sized room, adorned with images of the convent's sponsors, various clergy, and Saint Ējmiatsin on the walls. There, they serve delicious tea. The priest who celebrated the liturgy, Father Arsen Bagratuni, informs me about the foundation of the convent and other events, which he has started to gather and put in writing, for the convent has no official record about its past.

It is believed that the foundation of the convent was in 1650. It has seven cells, one salon, one dining hall, and other annexes. Next to the building stands the chapel, situated under a pointed arch supported by four large pillars, around which there are narrow, elongated windows. That chapel was renovated in 1728 with funds provided by Prince Melik' Minishk'arbash[181] agha Melik'ashkharhbekyan[182], that is Pehput'eants'. It was rebuilt in 1876 with 25,000 roubles, of which Pehput'ean gave 5,000, and the other 20,000 came from general fundraising.

There are 18 nuns in the convent, of whom 12 are *ordained archdeaconesses*. They are:

Duchess Abbess Katarinē Arghut'ean Erkaynabazuk,
Duchess Eprosinē Abamelik'eants',
Duchess Anna Khochaminaseants',
Duchess Sofi Amatuneats',
P'ep'ronē Khupeants',
Manya Loris-Melik'eants',
Gayanē Shahnazareants',
Hṛip'simē T'ahireants',
Ustianē Abeleants',
Shushanik Kharazean,
Iskuhi Ēnfiecheants',
Elmonya Parut'cheants'.

Almost all of them have personal allowances, which they use for their individual needs and the needs of the institution. The six *dpruhi*s are:

---

181 Minishkar Agha or Minishkar Bash: "bash" and "agha" were the noble titles of the princely family of the Behbut'eants'. See Khuts'ean, *T'iflisi S. Step'anos kusanats' anapati patmut'iwnĕ*, p. 16.

182 This name must be due to a misunderstanding or misspelling: it should be Melik'-Ashkharbek Behbut'eants'.

Nonya Tsoveneants', Ep'imya Vardanenants', Mariam T'almaseants', Hṛip'simē Ghoneants', Katarinē Kulusheants', Gayanē Alikhanenats'.

The annual revenue of the convent is 3,000 roubles, which is primarily generated from the estates, church donations, and gifts.

As far as I can recall, there are three Armenian establishments for nuns: one in Jerusalem, the second in Shushi (Karabakh), and the third one is this convent of St Step'anos, which I described here.[183] The convent of Shushi provides free education to, I believe, 6-7 girls. I do not know how the Jerusalem one serves the broader community's needs. The nuns from Tbilisi serve their wider community by bringing grace with their presence and beautiful singing during the funerals of wealthy Armenians, for which they are generously rewarded.

As much as I cherish this peaceful and holy institution, I assign fault to the nuns for remaining indifferent in this big city and for failing to reciprocate the public generosity in any way. Is it not accurate to say that those nuns were able, and even had the moral responsibility, to become carers for the sick, teachers, doctors, and consolers of the destitute during pandemics, or in their hearts, they could discover an alternative way to express the existence of their humble philanthropic sentiments? It would not hinder them from remaining pure, especially since they would become the purest ...[184]

Along with open admiration for the nuns of St Step'anos's Convent of Tbilisi, this article expressed disappointment that they only brought grace to the funerals of wealthy individuals in order to secure some revenue, and did not undertake any other public mission.[185] However, a lengthy letter[186] written in around 1850 by the abbess of St Step'anos's Convent, deaconess Gayanē Behbut'eants', to the abbess of St Katarinē's Convent of New Julfa, deaconess Eghisabeth Martiroseants', testified the following:

Those helpless orphan girls, who are left entirely unprotected, find a temporary refuge in the convent. Some of them get married and receive a modest dowry from the convent.[187]

---

183 The author must have been unaware of St Katarinē's Convent of New Julfa.
184 Bēylik'chean, "Awag sarkawaguhiner hay kusastanneri mej", *Hayrenik' Ōragir*, p. 2 and Bēylik'chean, "Awag sarkawaguhiner hay kusastanneri mej", *Hay Khōsnak*, pp. 79-82.
185 It is necessary to address this serious issue at a later time.
186 See Bishop Sargis Jalaleants', *Chanaparhordut'iwn i Metsn Hayastan* (A Journey to Greater Armenia), Vol. II, Tbilisi, 1858, pp. 61-68.
187 Ibid.

From this, it becomes apparent that, even though the nuns of St Stepʻanos's Convent of Tbilisi did not assume any significant public and philanthropic responsibility, they were at least busy taking care of orphans or providing shelter to helpless Armenian girls: they would care for the girls until adulthood and, after giving them into marriage, also offered them "a modest dowry".

On 5 December 1828, in her response to Archbishop Nersēs Ashtaraketsʻi regarding the financial performance of the convent of St Stepʻanos, Abbess Yustianē detailed other ways the nuns raised funds, and mentioned that besides the revenue from some of the estates, they also visited the houses of relatives on the eve of Christmas, sang the *sharakan* "Khorhurd Mets" (Great Mystery), announced the good tidings of Christ's birth, sang psalms for the deceased, and received financial rewards for their services.[188]

Abbess Yustianē also prepared another report for the Armenian Primate of Georgia, Archbishop Nersēs Ashtaraketsʻi, which sheds some light on the internal organisation of the congregation.

Alas, this is not a set of monastic rules, as we observed in the case of St Katarinē's Convent of New Julfa. Nevertheless, it is of equal significance for the study of the history of the Armenian female hermitages.

1. At the beginning of the divine betrothal, they usually ask the person who, constrained by the love of God, leaves his daughter for betrothal here with the immortal bridegroom, Christ, whether she is well-instructed and chaste, and whether she has earnestly been nurtured in sweetness of temper. In which pursuits has she excelled more, in spiritual or manual ones? Do her parents exhibit conduct that is virtuous enough? Was she consecrated to God in her childhood, or were there other factors or causes for her devotion? If these qualities are found in the young virgin, who is preparing to join us, in a spiritual way of life we receive her willingly with love, and we gradually begin to direct her mind towards our life of continence; then, little by little we engage her in the study of the divine scriptures which are useful and beneficial in finding eternal life and that which is pleasing to God, until we bring her to perfection, with which she will soon become worthy to receive the holy office of the Archdeaconate.

2. Overall, there are about fifteen persons in the convent. The hermitage cannot increase its number more than that: firstly, because of the limitations of the living space; secondly, to ensure a sincere and peaceful coexistence and way of life, given that they come from different families and generations. For even children from the same marriage are not in perfect harmony and love, let

---

188 See Khutsʻean, *Tʻiflisi S. Stepʻanos kusanatsʻ anapati patmutʻiwnĕ*, p. 40.

alone those born strangers to each other; they learn to unite and lead a life filled with love and honest labour without confusion and disorder.

3. Each individual brings money from their parents for living expenses based on their ability. And some bring it with them when they first come, others at ordination, while others pay only two *t'umans* yearly for the price of bread and secure their own vestments themselves. Those who do not possess any of these means, whose parents initially promised to provide a sufficient amount but find themselves unable to pay, are supported by the abbess herself using the assets of the hermitage and the wealthy nuns. All the property and income of this hermitage are under her authority, including the money of the nuns, whose needs, both in terms of food and clothing, are also catered for by her. Alongside the revenues, the expenses required for the maintenance and needs of the church, for the household, the orchards, and shops owned by the hermitage, if one of the nuns who has money falls sick, it is the Mother Superior who manages the expenses of the doctor and the medications by using the available funds.

4. If a financially self-sufficient virgin is under the yoke of the diaconate, neither she nor anyone from her family has the right to reappropriate or touch the money, either during her lifetime or thereafter. While she is alive, she oversees it, but upon her death, the expenses for her funeral are made from this fund according to the custom, whereas the hermitage inherits the remainder without engaging in any deception. And if she is not under the yoke [of the diaconate], while she is alive, the above stipulation applies, but after her death, the hermitage returns half of the funds to her parents and deploys the other half to cover the funeral expenses. However, if anyone in the community rebels and demands her money, which has never happened before, her ecclesiastical rank will be revoked, and she will be expelled from the hermitage in lay clothing, and it will be impossible to readmit her.

5. Anyone who wishes to go to her father's or relatives' house for urgent business or any other reason first obtains approval from the abbess. If the abbess then decides that her going is justified, she allows her a specified amount of time. If not, she prohibits her from leaving the hermitage, and she may not dare to get upset or feel despondent without informing anyone; she must address the abbess, and if she ignores them, to the community, and if they do not help either, then as befitting for the monastic life, she should bear her troubles in silence. And if she cannot endure it for a long time, the statutes do not forbid her to present to the spiritual governing body her pain alone without various scandalising details. According to our code of practice, to which she is already committed, it is not permitted to provide information to

the spiritual governing body before informing the abbess or the monastic community.

6. The care of everyone is the same. But if anyone is crowned with greater civility and chastity than her companions, fasts, is adorned with modest spiritual conduct, and is always clad in the awe of God, then, being a model for the others, the abbess holds them in particular esteem and care, be it in private or by public display. Those accused of minor misdemeanours receive the abbess's gentle admonition. If she is found guilty of more serious sins, she is brought before the spiritual governing body and undergoes a severe penance proportional to her fault.

7. Each should be valiant and vigilant in her good deeds and alert to evil. She should strive to earn a reputation for purity by her virtuous behaviour. If anything happens and a minor disagreement arises, they should promptly reconcile before it reaches the abbess. Dedication to private prayer depends on the individual's wish and inclination; there is no pressure in this respect. However, during general prayer, they are to be awake at dawn willingly, without perturbation, with a pure heart, and stand before the holy altar, with humble veneration, singing the psalms, alternatively with their companions. In compliance with the cannons of every church, the morning service begins with all the community kneeling and the midday office, too, if it is pleasing to people. After completing this hour's celebration, they sing the remaining psalms. Then, with prayer on their lips, each of them goes to their rooms, having first extended their greeting to the abbess. After that, they sometimes begin their handiwork, the benefits and usefulness of which they decide independently. Sometimes, they occupy themselves with reading the Holy Scriptures, and then the abbess holds them privately in esteem. No one can stay there without participating in prayer and services except for illness or other justifiable causes. The individual rooms are for the most revered nuns and communal space for the others.

8. On ordinary days, the food is first prepared in the refectory, and then the nuns enter along with the abbess, and each stands at her place around the table until Grace is said. Then they sit with decorum and silently enjoy a standard meal without any distinction in food between the old and the young. The dishes are prepared to suit the day: sometimes there happen to be two and other times three types, sometimes more, sometimes less. Moreover, everything we practise is the same for the young and the old alike.

9. In the evening, they begin with vespers, according to the custom of all churches, then with the peace hour chant, concluding with common prayer and singing the eighth psalm, "In my distress" [Ps. 119 (120)], in pairs as before. At night, after partaking in a similar meal, they collectively recite the

"Let there be" and, affectionately bidding each other farewell, they retire to rest with vigilance and prudence, practising moderate sleep, but not throughout the night.[189]

Bishop Mkrtich' Aghawnuni, in his work "Miabank' ew ayts'eluk' hay Erusaghēmi" (Monks and Visitors of Armenian Jerusalem), recalled that the abbesses of Tbilisi's St Step'anos's Convent were among the visitors on a pilgrimage tof the Holy Land and the monastery of St James, and that they held the rank of deaconesses. Had the tradition of female diaconate been non-existent or an antireligious phenomenon, it would be difficult to imagine that the overseer of Jerusalem's St James monastery would have hosted them or at least mentioned their ecclesiastical rank.

KATARINĒ GHORGHANOV (DEACONESS): One of the nuns of Tbilisi's female hermitage, undertook a pilgrimage to visit the monastery of St James, in the reign of patriarch Yovhannēs Movsēsean, two times in 1864, and, on this occasion, she donated to the monastery of St James 31 chasubles crafted from red brocade adorned with gold embroidery, silver candlesticks, and so on. She also donated an olive field with the appropriate legal paperwork.[190]

HRIP'SIMĒ VIRGIN T'AHIREANTS' OF TBILISI: Born in 1847. In 1874, she was ordained as a deaconess in St Step'anos's Convent of Tbilisi. With the "Letter of Blessing" of patriarch Yarut'iwn, for the benefit of paying the debts of the monastery of St James, she was appointed as the treasurer of the donations, and for that purpose, she collected donations. Deaconess Hrip'simē and Sōfia Step'anean, a widow from Shushi, embarked on a pilgrimage to the monastery of St James, and deaconess Hrip'simē brought donations of 3,000 roubles and gave it to the patriarch, and, in 1894, she was rewarded with a cross adorned with diamond and containing a relic of St Hrip'simē.

Using her own money, Hrip'simē T'ayireants' also had a large, magnificent, gold-painted patriarchal veil made, which she presented to the monastery of St Ējmiatsin. This same veil is paraded by the officials in front of the Catholicos of all Armenians during special celebrations.[191]

---

189 Ibid., pp. 41-46.

190 Aghawnuni, Mkrtich', *Miabank' ew ayts'eluk' hay Erusaghēmi* (Monks and Visitors of Armenian Jerusalem), Jerusalem, 1929, p. 183.

191 Ibid., pp. 225-226.

The above informs us of both the date of birth and ordination of this virtuous and influential archdeaconess, Hṛipʻsimē Tʻayireantsʻ.[192] The deaconesses' devoted mission and the material offerings from her give us direct insight into the glory of the recent past, as well as the pure and prayerful labour of godly virgins who took part in our church life, and stood on the altar of our faith with their hierarchical rank.

Today, several of their gifts donated to the monastery of Ējmiatsin – the painting of the Ējmiatsin cathedral gifted to Catholicos Khrimyan Hayrik (1820-1907), a beautiful needlework adorned with silver threads, and the wooden doors of the Mother Church – are preserved in the Mother See, in the old residence of the Catholicos.[193]

---

192 She passed away in the year 1934 and was buried in the clergy cemetery of the St Gayianē church.

193 St Stepʻanos's Convent of Tbilisi and the community of nuns living there came to the attention of English-speaking audiences through the travel notes of the British traveller Henry Lynch. Lynch met Hṛipʻsimē Tʻayireantsʻ in Ējmiatsin on 26 September 1893, during the inauguration and the anointment ceremony of Catholicos Khrimyan Hayrik (Lynch has "October", which must nevertheless be considered the result of confusion or typo). Lynch does not mention her name but refers to her as "a nun from Tiflis". He writes that the nun was present in the upper chambers of the pontifical residence with other prominent guests: "The nun is a charming woman, and we make great friends. She informs me that she is almost an unique specimen of her order; the convent at Tiflis is perhaps a solecism. Nunneries are not popular with the Armenians. I think my reader may appreciate the magnificent robes which belong to her office, and of which, by her kindness, I am able to supply an illustration" (Lynch, Henry F.B., *Armenia: Travels and Studies*, Vol. I, The Russian Provinces, London, 1901, pp. 252-253). Archdeaconess Hṛipʻsimē Tʻayireantsʻ gave Lynch one of the photographs of herself in a full ceremonial dress taken in Jerusalem. The caption under the photograph reproduced in Lynch's book does not contain the name of the depicted individual, and it solely reads "Armenian Nun". Relying on the information provided by Mkrtichʻ Aghawnuni, in the Western Armenian version of the present book, we mistakenly assumed that Hṛipʻsimē Tʻayireantsʻ's photograph of the deaconess in a full ceremonial dress had been taken in 1894 in Jerusalem. However, she gave this same photograph to Lynch in Ējmiatsin in 1893. Knowing the date of birth of Hṛipʻsimē Tʻayireantsʻ (1847), even if the picture was taken in 1893, she would have been 46 years old. Yet, a careful look at the photograph suggests that she was much younger in it. Moreover, the columns seen in the background of the deaconess look very similar to the columns of St Stepʻanos's church of Tbilisi. Consequently, the photograph was most likely taken in 1874 in Tbilisi on the occasion of Hṛipʻsimē Tʻayireantsʻ's ordination as deaconess when she was only 27 years old.

Years ago, when I visited the community of Gayianeants' Sisters, created under the aegis of the "T'ṛch'nots' Boyn" (Birds' Nest) orphanage in the Lebanese town of Jebeil Byblos, I had the joy of meeting the deaconess sister Hṛip'simē Sasunean there. On this occasion, along with other material, she gave me another copy of Archdeaconess Hṛip'simē T'ayireants''s photograph mentioned earlier. Most likely, Hṛip'simē T'ayireants' had more than one copy of this photograph, one of which she passed on to the English traveller Lynch in Ējmiatsin. The original copy of the photograph used in the present edition is in our possession.

In addition, it is necessary to mention here another important piece of evidence provided by Nicolas Zernov (1898-1980) in his "The Western Dispersion of the Armenian Church". Zernov was born in Moscow into the family of a representative of the Russian Orthodox intelligentsia. In 1917, when the Bolsheviks overthrew the tsar, the Zernov family found refuge in Tbilisi, in the independent Republic of Georgia, until 1920. It was during this brief period that Nicolas Zernov had the opportunity to visit St Step'anos's Convent of Tbilisi and meet its nuns. Of this, he wrote: "They (i.e. the Armenians) have kept the diaconate open to women, a practice which fell gradually into desuetude among other Eastern Christians and disappeared altogether in the twelfth century" (Zernov, Nicolas, "The Western Dispersion of the Armenian Church", *The Church Quarterly Review* 129, 1939, pp. 251-266, pp. 255-256; see also Corley, Felix, "Zernov and the Armenian Deaconesses of Tiflis", 2022, p. 5, <https://www.academia.edu/83293238/>, accessed on 18 January 2024). In the footnote to this, Zernov added: "I was personally present at the Eucharist in the Armenian Church of St Stephen in Tiflis in 1920, where a woman deacon fully vested brought forward the chalice for the communion of the people" (ibid., n. 8).

In another work dedicated to the religious life of Tbilisi, Zernov wrote: "Besides Russian churches, the Georgian capital had its own ancient cathedrals, including the magnificent Sioni Cathedral. The difference between the Georgian and Russian forms of devoutness was a complete surprise for us, as until that point, we considered the latter to be the only true Orthodoxy. We found even more unusual forms of ecclesiastical life among the Armenians. Open altars, original, very melodious singing, colourful eastern vestments – all of this drew our attention. Several times, we had been in the church of the female convent; there were deaconesses who took part in the service. They had marvellous vestments; there were white veils on their heads reaching the edge of their robes. Similar to deacons, they would present the Holy Chalice for communion. Their example convinced me that women can successfully participate in liturgical services" (Zernov, Nicolas (ed.), *Na Perelome: Tri Pokoleniia Odnoi Moskovskoi Sem'i (Semeynaia Khronika Zernovykh) (1812-1921)* (At the Breaking Point: Three Generations of One Moscow Family (The Family Chronicle of the Zernovs) [1812-1921]), Paris, 1970, pp. 403-404; see also Corley, "Zernov and the Armenian Deaconesses of Tiflis").

On the main door, we can read the following inscription: "Memory: Archdeaconess Hṛipʻsimē Aghekʻ[194] Tʻayireantsʻ; 1338[195] (= 1889)." A small inscription slightly below this reveals that it was made in Tbilisi by "Ingenieur Nicolas Grigorian". It is highly symbolic and touching that whenever we enter the Mother Cathedral of Holy Ējmiatsin to kneel, worship, and renew our covenant at the altar of the Holy Descent, we realise that we enter the temple through doors which were gifted by a luminous soul, Archdeaconess Hṛipʻsimē Tʻayireantsʻ, the abbess of St Stepʻanos's Convent of Tbilisi.

In addition to the above evidence, in 1912, "Ararat," the official monthly magazine of the patriarchal see of Holy Ējmiatsin, mentioned the following in the list of donations:

> The abbess of St Stepʻanos's Convent of Tbilisi, Archdeaconess Hṛipʻsimē Tʻayireantsʻ, has donated to the Mother Cathedral two veils with silver-threaded tassels for the vessel of the patriarchal anointment and the holy myrrh.[196]

---

194 In his important volume dedicated to the epigraphic heritage of Vagharshapat, Arsen Harutʻyunyan adds a second surname "Aghekʻ[sandryan]" to the name of the deaconess (see Harutʻyunyan, Arsen, *Vagharshapat: Vankʻerě ew vimagru-tʻyunnerě* (Vagharshapat: The Monasteries and the Epigraphic Data), Holy Ēj-miatsin, 2016, p. 90).

195 Besides this date of the Armenian calendar, there is a year 4381 carved twice in the shape of a cross in the centre of the door. In this case, we should not consider the calculations based on the Armenian Era of 551, but the Primary Armenian or the Haykean calendar: 4381-1889=2492 (BCE), which is the start date of the Primary Armenian calendar marking the victory of the eponymous patriarch of the Armenians Hayk over Bel. Regarding this, see Harutʻyunyan, *Vagharshapat: Vankʻerě ew vimagrutʻyunnerě*, p. 91.

196 Editors, "Mayr Atʻoṛ" (Mother See), *Ararat* 10-11, 1912, p. 1051. Similar information is found in "Koys H. Tʻayireani Nuērě" (The Gift of Nun H. Tʻayirean), *Lumay* (3, 1903, p. 271): "Nun H. Tʻayirean's gift: on the occasion of the forthcoming blessing of the myrrh, the virtuous nun Hṛipʻsimē Tʻayirean personally financed a wonderful and golden-crafted large patriarchal veil, which is carried in front of the Catholicos of All Armenians during prominent church ceremonies."

Mother Cathedral of St Ējmiatsin: Silver- and gold-threaded needlework; gift from the nuns of St Step'anos's Convent of Tbilisi; Ējmiatsin, the old residence of the Catholicos.

Mother Cathedral of St Ējmiatsin carved in wood; Gift from the humble virgin Hrip'simē T'ayireants'; Inscription: "To the Eagle of Vaspurakan, our Armenian Father, the Supreme Patriarch and Catholicos of All Armenians, Mkrtich' I, from the humble virgin Hrip'simē T'ayireants'."
Below: "1893, Sep. Ējmiatsin." Ējmiatsin, the old residence of the Catholicos.

The main door of the Mother Cathedral of St Ējmiatsin. Gift from Archdeaconess Ḥṛip'simē T'ayireants'; Inscription: "Memory: Archdeaconess Ḥṛip'simē Aghek' T'ayireants'; 1338 (= 1889)." Below: "Ingenieur Nicolas Grigorian."

It is evident that the above mentioned donation was made on 30 September 1912, in Holy Ējmiatsin on the occasion of the grand ceremony for the blessing of the Holy Myrrh by the hand of the Catholicos of All Armenians Gēorg V. It was attended by nine nuns from St Step'anos's Convent of Tbilisi led by their Mother Superior Hrip'simē T'ayireants'. This historical fact is significant by itself, as it demonstrates that deaconesses in the Armenian church were not isolated in their nunneries or detached from the rest of the world. Instead, they maintained an impressive presence in the social and national-ecclesiastical events. Here is what the monthly magazine "Ararat" reported about the ceremony mentioned above:

> For most pilgrims, the presence on the altar of nine nuns who came from Tiflis is of some interest. Dressed in church vestments and wearing stoles, they served during the entire liturgy, fanning the flabella under the leadership of the Mother Superior Hrip'simē T'ayireants'. Of them Khōjaminasean, Ermonia Bērut'ch'ean, Mariam Dōlmazean, Katarinē Guloyean were standing on the right, while Kharazean Shushanik, Ep'emia Vardanean, Hrip'simē Ghonean, and Gayeanē Alikhanean were on the left.[197]

To further establish facts about the social presence of deaconesses, let us not forget to mention the nuns from Tbilisi who arrived in the Mother See of Holy Ējmiatsin on 25 October 1953 for the feast of the Exaltation of the Holy Cross. The 1953 text, entitled "Mayr At'orum", references this as below:

> On that day, three respectable deaconesses, nuns from Tbilisi's St Gēorg church came on a pilgrimage to the Mother See of Holy Ējmiatsin and participated in the celebration of the Divine Liturgy.[198]

Unfortunately, it was impossible for us to verify the identities of these three deaconesses. Were these "three respectable deaconesses, nuns from Tbilisi's St Gēorg church," originally deaconesses from St Step'anos's Convent or nuns

---

197 Aw. H., "Hay keank' ew ekeghets'i: Norin Vehap'arut'iwn T.T. Gēorg V Amenayn Hayots' Kat'oghikosi anuanakoch'ut'iwnĕ, Gēorgean H. chemarani tōnĕ ew s. Miwrōni ōrhnutiwnĕ" (Armenian Life and Church: The Adoption of the Name of His Holiness Supreme Patriarch and Catholicos of All Armenians Gēorg V, the Feast of the Gēvorgyan Theological Seminary, and the Blessing of the Holy Myrrh), *Ararat* 10-11, 1912, pp. 879-891; p. 888. During the dinner that took place after the Divine Liturgy and the ceremony of the blessing of the Holy Myrrh, it was proposed to raise a glass to "the Armenian virgins" who had contributed to the service (see ibid., p. 890).

198 Editors, "Mayr At'orum" (In the Mother See), *Ējmiatsin* 10, 1953, pp. 15-16; p. 16.

from St Gēorg church who were merely in pastoral service? It seems that after Georgia's Sovietisation, St Step'anos's Convent must have been affected by the soviet propaganda of atheism.[199] The convent might have been nationalised or simply closed, as a result of which the nuns may have been forced to continue their spiritual service in pastoral churches such as St Gēorg. Here, we are still dealing with conjectures, and are hoping for more comprehensive research in the future to clarify this.[200]

However, there is evidence that in the 1930s, Archdeaconess Nunē Vermishyan of St Step'anos's church of Tbilisi served during the Sunday services at the Armenian parish church of Tbilisi's Jgrashen village. In March 1930, Bishop Artak Smbatyants', the Primate of the Armenian Diocese in Georgia, granted the request of the parish council of Jgrashen village in Tbilisi, and asked Catholicos Gēorg V to bestow the right to wear a pectoral cross on deaconess Nunē Vermishyan in honor of her long service.[201]

> The former nun of the nunnery of St Step'anos's church of Tbilisi, the modestly radiating Archdeaconess virgin Nunē Artemyan-Vermishyan, who has led an angelic life, who had served in the mentioned hermitage since her

---

199 During the era of Soviet atheistic propaganda, the Soviet authorities undertook a harsh stance against all religious institutions, resulting in the confiscation and destruction of numerous churches and monasteries. Consequently, many virgin deaconesses were left without their former residences and places of worship. For further exploration of this topic, refer to Mkrtch'yan's work, "Kusanats' lk'vats anapatneri sarkavaguhinerĕ".

200 Bishop Derenik Polatean, one of the members of the congregation of the Armenian Catholicosate of the Great House of Cilicia, visited Tbilisi on 12 October 1953, and on this occasion, he published his impressions in the "Hask" (Ear of Corn) magazine. He wrote: "In the morning I visit the Armenian deaconesses. There are three of them: Hṙip'simē Ghonean, Katarinē Gulozean, and Nunē Vermishean. They do not have a separate nunnery" (see Derenik Polatean, "Ugheworut'iwn i S. Ējmiatsin" (Journey to Holy Ējmiatsin), *Hask* 1, 1954, pp. 9-23; p. 16). It is joyous to see the photograph of the mentioned three deaconesses on the same page; however, it is impossible not to see a deep sadness in their eyes, the sunset of their dedication and the extinguishing of their cast-in-gold dream. It is evident that nothing remains of their glorious nunnery. The Soviet authorities of the time confiscated everything, and the virgin deaconesses found themselves without their former residence and place of prayer. Regarding this, see also Mkrtch'yan, "Kusanats' lk'vats anapatneri sarkavaguhinerĕ."

201 Artak Smbatyants', *Vaweragrer Hay ekeghets'u patmut'ean* (Documents of the History of the Armenian Church), Vol. III, Yerevan, 1997, p. 39. See also Mkrtchyan, "Sarkavaguhineri tsaṙayut'yunn u pashtonĕ Hay aṙak'elakan ekeghets'um", p. 50.

childhood and today continues to serve with holiness, modesty, resolute self-devotedness, and vigilance, received the holy office of archdeaconess in 1914. However, owing to *the adverse circumstances of the time*, until today, she has not been awarded the pectoral cross, which she fully deserves.

The mentioned same virgin Nunē has been serving in our St Avetyats' church of Jgrashen during the Divine Liturgy every Sunday in the holy office of archdeaconess for four years, with which she generates great spiritual motivation among the pious parishioners and in the hearts and souls of churchgoers, and she, simultaneously, brings profound gratitude and satisfaction even to visitors of different faiths and attendees of the Divine Liturgy.

Therefore, acknowledging the merits of the mentioned modestly radiating virgin Nunē Artemyan-Vermishyan, this church council humbly appeals to Your Supreme Holiness and most humbly requests You, oh Holy Father, who inspires and values worthy clerics, to be kind and bestow the pectoral cross on the devout virgin Nunē to encourage her to continue her lengthy, impeccable, self-devoted, and most diligent service. [202]

In the request, the expression "the former nun of the nunnery" used by Bishop Artak Smbatyants' further confirms the suggestion made earlier that St Step'anos's Convent, along with numerous other religious establishments, became a victim of the Soviet propaganda of atheism and even of the repressions of the time. This would likely have been the reason why the nuns continued their spiritual service outside nunneries in the communal parish churches, which the Soviet authorities somehow tolerated. In this request from the Primate to the Catholicos, the phrase "the adverse circumstances of the time" also hints at the antireligious sentiments of the period. It is likely this that hindered Nunē Artemyan-Vermishyan, from receiving commensurate appreciation from the Catholicos. However, she was so strongly devout that she likely did not need such appreciation to continue her spiritual duties.

There is evidence that St Step'anos's Convent and its virgin nuns, under the leadership of their abbess, survived until the 1920s. After which, as a consequence of the open antireligious repressions by the Soviet authorities, the nuns dispersed, and many of them found themselves in difficult moral and financial circumstances. As with the previously mentioned virgin Nunē Sargsyan and Abbess Hṛip'simē, [203] it is hard not to be moved when reading

---

202 Smbatyants', *Vaweragrer Hay ekeghets'u patmut'ean*, pp. 497-498. See also Mkrtch-yan, "Sarkavaguhineri tsaṛayut'yunn u pashtonĕ Hay aṛak'elakan ekeghets'um", pp. 50-51.

203 See above, note 105.

the appeal of Archdeaconess T'ayireants', which she sent to Catholicos Gēorg V on 24 May 1927:

> It has long been known to Your Holy Council that Tbilisi's ancient nunnery is not in its former luminous and secure state due to the latest political developments: the apartments of the convent have been seized, the nuns have dispersed and found refuge some with relatives, others with their parents, while some, with the support of acquaintances, teetering on the edge of destitution, barely manage to make ends meet. As for me, the unfortunate one, deprived of parents and relatives, in my old age and poor health, I barely survive in great despair by appealing to various acquaintances. Many times, my torments and destitution have even pushed me to commit suicide and end my constantly suffering soul and tormented existence, but, considering my name and rank, I have endeavoured to get rid of those dishonourable thoughts. Today, my past is better known to You, Supreme Father, and Your Holy Council than to anyone else, but being also forgotten by You, I suffer from extreme poverty and am forced to turn to begging. Holy Fathers, a few months ago, I heard that, taking into account my situation, Your Council decided to invite me to Ējmiatsin, provide me with a piece of bread and a dwelling place, and enable me to spend the last days of my life without perturbation. Now, months have passed since that day, and I continue to live in the same destitution, and there is an arrangement in this regard. With this appeal, I am now requesting that if there are any hindrances to my move to Ējmiatsin, you appoint me a monthly pension, which will enable me to navigate on the edge of destitution. I humbly ask you also to inform His Holiness.
>
> Abbess Hṛip'simē T'ayireants'.[204]

It is interesting to observe here the attention and effort of high-ranking clergy who, sensing the gradual extinguishing of the church's ancient office of deaconesses, endeavoured to do everything possible to keep the last shining sparks of the still burning wick of faith alive. To that end, The Mother See set up a monthly payment of 15 roubles to Nunē and Hṛip'simē, the deaconesses of the convent of Shushi, while Archdeaconess Hṛip'simē T'ayireants' was brought to Holy Ējmiatsin, where she lived until she died in 1934.[205]

---

204 Kharatyan, "T'bilisii S. Step'anos kusanats' anapati ew mayrpet ishkhanuhi Hṛip'-simē T'ayireants'i masin", p. 89.

205 The Mother See set up a monthly payment of 15 roubles to Nunē and Hṛip'simē, the deaconesses of the convent of Shushi, whereas Archdeaconess Hṛip'simē T'ayireants' was brought to Holy Ējmiatsin, where she lived until she died in 1934, and was buried in the clergy cemetery of Ējmiatsin, near St Gayianē church (see ibid., p. 91). The inscription on her tombstone reads: "ABBESS OF TBILISI'S

Needlework gonfalon. Inscription: "This is a souvenir from Mnats'akan from Yere-van to Hrip'simē, the daughter of Gethsemane, at the door of the church of St Paul and St Peter." Ējmiatsin, treasury.

ST STEP'ANOS'S CONVENT PRINCESS HRIP'SIMĒ T'AYIREANTS'" (see Harut'yunyan, *Vagharshapat: Vank'erě ew vimagrut'yunnerě*, p. 319).

Congregation of "Galfayean National Orphanage of Presentation of the Holy Virgin at the Age of Three" in Constantinople

In addition to the remarkable nunneries mentioned earlier, there were also others in Armenian diasporic centres, such as Constantinople and Lebanon. Under the auspices of the Armenian patriarchate in Turkey, Srbuhi Nshan-Galfayean[206] founded the congregation of "Galfayean National Orphanage of Presentation of the Holy Virgin at the Age of Three" in 1866. Like others, this institution also had a national-ecclesiastical spiritual structure, with the nuns receiving ranks up to the level of archdeaconess. It is worth noting here the names of the blessed high-ranking clergy who, in solemn church ceremonies, conferred the rank of deacon or subdeacon on the sisters of the congregation: Archbishop Step'anos Aghawni (twice elected as patriarch), Archbishop Gabriēl Chēwahirchean[207] (patriarchal *locum tenens* of the same See), Archbishop Mesrop Naroyean, Archbishop Garegin Khach'aturean, Archbishop Shnork' Galustean, and Archbishop Sahak Mashalean.

A booklet prepared for the 60th anniversary of the Galfayean nunnery, which effectively presents the history of this institution, provides the following details:

> To show appreciation for the work of the Galfayean Sisters and to encourage them further, in 1918, on the occasion of the *Tearnĕndaraj* [Candlemas Day], Archbishop Gabriēl Chēwahirchean, on the day having the title of the *locum tenens* of the Catholicos and Patriarch, consecrated the praying area of the orphanage as a chapel, with the privilege of serving the Divine Liturgy there, and bestowed the rank of deaconess on the Mother of the orphanage and three Sisters.[208]

---

206 For the biography of Srbuhi Nshan-Galfayean, see Grigor Margarean, *Kensagrut'iwn Srbuhi Mayrapeti Nshan-Galfayean. Himnadir-mayr hamanun orbanots'i aghjkants' hastateal i Khasgiwgh 1 Yunuar 1866* (Biography of the Abbess Srbuhi Nshan-Galfayean: Mother-Founder of the Homonymous Girls' Orphanage established in Khasgiwgh on 1 January 1866), Constantinople, 1892.

207 See Mkrtch'yan, "Sarkavaguhineri tsarayut'yunn u pashtonĕ Hay Arak'elakan Ekeghets'um", p. 47.

208 See *Vat'sunameak (1866-1926) Galfayean aghjkants' orbanots'i* (60th Anniversary (1866-1926) of the Galfayean Girls' Orphanage), Khasgiwgh, p. 24 (the booklet does not have the place and date of the publication). This same information, with some additions, was confirmed later with the following supplementary details added to the same passage: "On the same day, Mother K'ristinē, Sisters Aghawni, Mariam, and Newrik. They were granted the ranks of teachers and the privilege

When Abbess deaconess K'ristinē P'ap'azean passed away in 1919, she was succeeded by Abbess Aghawni K'ēōsēean. Regarding her appointment, the following compelling details have been preserved:

> After the burial ceremony [of Abbess deaconess K'ristinē P'ap'azean] and the funeral reception, with the unanimous decision of His Beatitude Patriarch [Zawēn I Tēr-Eghiayean] and the present representatives of the national authorities, the *locum tenens* of the deceased, Abbess Aghawni K'ēōsēean was appointed as the Abbess of the orphanage. [...] Then, through a special ceremony, His Grace the Patriarch put the stole on the shoulder of the newly elected Mother and passed onto her the abbatial cross and ring, after which the clergy sang the *sharakan* of virgins *Andzink' nuirealk'* (Devoted Souls).[209]

This evidence indicates that the Armenian clergy in Constantinople were generally open-minded towards nuns and, more specifically, deaconesses who held a clerical rank. Not only did the high-ranking clergy value their self-devoted service in the national-ecclesiastical life by bestowing on them various ecclesiastical privileges, they also supported them in effectuating their vows of service. As such, on 27 December 1923, the Catholicos of All Armenians Gēorg V, with a patriarchal decree, granted the earlier mentioned deaconess Aghawni K'ēōsēean the right to wear a pectoral cross, while in 1933, the Patriarch of Constantinople, Archbishop Mesrop Naroyean, bestowed on her the rank of archdeaconess and with it the right to perform all the services conducted by deacons in the church.

> On 24 November 1933, through the consecration by His Beatitude the Patriarch, two Sisters received the four ranks of the office of notary and the privilege to wear a stole. With these ranks, they had the right to cense and read the Gospel during the liturgy, whereas Mother Aghawni was granted the right to conduct all the services assigned to deacons in the church. Mother Aghawni conducted the offertory during the liturgy, while the two Sisters who wore the stole censed the altar where they were called to serve.[210]

Mother Aghawni K'ēōsēean passed away in 1955 and was succeeded by her sister, Mariam K'ēōsēean. The account of the appointment of this virtuous Sister to the vacant seat of the Galfayean nunnery is touching. On the occasion

---

to wear a stole, each by an individual decree. On this occasion, His Grace Chēwahirchean also gave them the permission to wear a cross" (see *Galfayean aghjkants' orbanots' (1866-1934)* (Galfayean Girls' Orphanage [1866-1934]), Constantinople, 1935, pp. 48-49; no name of the author of the booklet is provided).

209 Ibid., p. 50.

210 See *Galfayean aghjkants' orbanots' (1866-1934)*, p. 66.

of this appointment, Patriarch Garegin Trapizonts'i performed a solemn ceremony, bestowing on her the rank of archdeaconess:

> [...] Before the Divine Liturgy, the Holy Father conferred the rank of subdeacon on Sister Mariam, who was dressed in a violet robe, with her fellows, Sister Zarmuhi and Sister Aruseak, standing next to her.
>
> His Beatitude gave her the stole in the middle of the song and *sharakan*. Before the greeting, the rank of deaconess was bestowed on Mariam with the *sharakan* "Urakh ler" (Rejoice). The Sister moved on her knees towards the altar, accompanied by two Sisters on her sides, with Father Aram as the officiating priest.
>
> Sister Mariam turned her face towards the public and stretched her hands upwards, symbolising the abandonment of all earthly matters. The *dpirs* sang "Arzhani ē" (She is worthy) three times.[211]

This account is noteworthy because Patriarch Khach'aturean performed the ordination of the deaconess using the canon of the ordination of deacons as preserved in the *Mayr Mashtots'*. Here too it becomes evident that the title of deaconess, bestowed through ordination, was not merely a blessing but, quite literally, a ceremonial enactment of mystery, with all its significance and ritual content.

Equally significant is the ceremony of the abbatial oath when Archdeaconess Aghawni K'ēōsēean had previously assumed the role of the Abbess of the Galfayean nunnery.

> I take an oath, bearing witness with the entirety of my essence, always to remain unwaveringly truthful to the will of the founder, Mother Srbuhi Galfayean of blessed memory, and never to stray from the directives she imparted, conscientiously and flawlessly executing her wishes, and endeavouring to effectuate the responsibilities entrusted to the humble me by the high command of the Patriarch, for the glory of God, and the benefit and prosperity of this sacred house.[212]

The Catholicos-Coadjutor Babgēn I Kiwlesērean (1868-1936), in his valuable study titled *Patmut'iwn Kat'oghikosats' Kilikioy* (History of the Catholicoi of Cilicia), made a reference to the ceremony of the blessing of the holy myrrh in the Mother Church of Antelias on 29 March 1936. The exiled Catholicosate

---

211 See Perch Ērziean, Ch'inar Yakob, *Haryurameay yishatakaran Galfayean tan 1866-1966* (The One Hundred Year Commemoration of the House of Galfayean 1866-1966), Istanbul, 1966, p. 56.

212 Ibid., p. 57.

of the Great House of Cilicia, which had been experiencing the gracious hospitality of the mirthful seashores of Antelias in Lebanon, was to bless its first holy myrrh by the hand of Catholicos Babgēn I Kiwlesērean., and simultaneously consecrate Antelias' estates. This significant national-ecclesiastical event was attended not only by the Primates of the Armenian Apostolic Church but also by thousands of pilgrims, including deaconesses:

> To be present as pilgrims at the ceremony of the Blessing of the Holy Myrrh, two sisters, Aghawni and Mariam, the Abbesses of the Galfayean orphanage, arrived in Antelias via the Constantinople–Aleppo line [...] Abbess Aghawni is an ordained deacon, and her sister, Mariam, is a *dpir*. Both served at the altar during the ceremony of the Blessing of the Holy Myrrh.[213]

> The Abbess of the Galfayean orphanage of Constantinople, deaconess Aghawni K'ēōsēean, and her sister, *dpruhi* Mariam, both in the vestments and stoles [...] The liturgy began, and when the time of the greeting approached, the procession returned to the Church of the Holy Translators to bring the vessel with the myrrh, sweet-scented oils, and the box of the Holy Arms. Deaconess Aghawni conducted the offertory, and *dpruhi* Mariam read the Gospel.[214]

These many events, all of which are related to our national-ecclesiastical life, serve as conclusive proof of the beneficial impact of the positive presence of deaconesses in the heart of the Armenian Church and the potential effectiveness of their devout activities. If today's clergy and that of the future chooses to treat them with open-mindedness and encouragement, then the journey of deaconesses may continue within the Armenian Church, perhaps even with the addition of new titles. Let us not disregard the fertility of this font that holds holy mystery, and which for centuries has given birth to our nuns and deaconesses.

The Sisters of this congregation in Lebanon showed selfless dedication, spiritually and self-devotedly serving the Holy Armenian Apostolic Church and the nation in general by educating, nurturing, and preparing for life hundreds of orphaned girls. To emphasise this dedication, we present here the monastic rule and programme of the national-ecclesiastical mission of the

---

213 See Mkrtch'yan, "Sarkavaguhineri tsaṛayut'yunn u pashtonĕ Hay Aṛak'elakan Ekeghets'um", pp. 49-50.

214 Babgēn Kiwlesērean, *Patmut'iwn Kat'oghikosats' Kilikioy. 1441-ēn minchew mer ōrerĕ* (History of the Catholicoi of Cilicia: From 1441 up to the Present Day), Antelias, 1939, col. 1073.

members of the Galfayean congregation in Constantinople, which was prepared and ratified by the founder of the nunnery, the late Srbuhi Nshan-
Galfayean, during her lifetime:

THE RULES OF THE ORPHANAGE FROM THE TESTAMENT OF ABBESS SRBUHI

Article 1: The orphanage has been established under the auspices of the Catholicos of All Armenians of Holy Ējmiatsin as a shelter and education centre
for the Armenian orphan girls, whose care is undertaken by orphan-nurturing female friends under the supervision of the Mother of the orphanage.

Article 2: The property and revenues of the orphanage are managed, and the
right to benefit from its care is exclusive to those orphans who have been
accepted and found shelter within it. They forfeit this right if they leave the
orphanage due to marriage, adoption by others, or securing a position else-
where.

Article 3: The property and the revenues of the orphanage are managed,
along with the orphans, by those Sisters who, out of love for orphans, have
dedicated themselves to nurturing and volunteered to take care of them, both
within the orphanage and outside it while carrying out the directives of the
overseeing Mother. They also forfeit this right if expelled or voluntarily leave
the Society of Orphan Nurturers.

Article 4: The Society of Orphan Nurturers consists of orphan-nurturing female friends, called Sisters, whose head is the Mother of the orphanage.

Article 5: Orphan-nurturing female friends or Sisters can be appointed to be
all those young ladies and widows who dedicate themselves to caring for the
orphans for free and who take an oath to comply fully with the rules of the
orphanage.

Article 6: Orphan-nurturing female friends can also be appointed from be
those orphans educated in the orphanage who are already twenty years of
age, who have had achievements in their education, and whose behaviour is
deemed worthy of joining the ranks of the female friends of the orphanage
by the overseeing Mother and her advisors. They immediately leave the ranks
of orphans, receive the name Sister, take the same oath, and receive the same
office and responsibilities as the Sisters who have been appointed from outside.

Article 7: Orphan-nurturing Sisters are free to break their oath and resign
their membership of the Society whenever they wish so. It will suffice to inform the Mother of the orphanage in writing one month in advance. Those

who ignore this condition and sneak out of the orphanage or leave it alto-gether are considered expelled from the Society and are thus announced by the overseeing Mother.

Article 8: Those female friends who do not comply with the rules of the or-phanage by breaking their oath are reprimanded two or three times and still do not correct their behaviour bring disrepute to the institution with their deviant behaviour, and after admonition do not reform, are expelled from the Society of Orphan Nurturers by the decision of the Mother and her advi-sors.

Article 9: The Mother of the orphanage is the head of the Society of Orphan Nurturers and the overseer of the orphanage.

Article 10: The tenure of the Mother's position in the orphanage extends un-til the end of her life, even if she is unable to perform her role due to illness or old age. Under these circumstances, upon the proposal of the general council of female friends, a *locum tenens* is chosen from among them, and she performs her duties in her [the Mother's] name and until the end of her [the Mother's] life.

Article 11: However, if the Mother of the orphanage fails in her role and breaks her oath, causing moral or material damage to the orphanage by her conduct or deeds, she must be indicted. The indictment is addressed to the Patriarch of Constantinople through the father confessor of the orphanage, who investigates it, and if the defendant fails to prove her innocence and does not reform after two or three admonitions, she is removed from her office by the Patriarch.

Article 12: If, for whatever reason, the office of the Mother of the orphanage is vacant, three female friend advisers assume the interim responsibilities of her role and form an emergency council of orphan-nurturing female friends for the elections of the successor. To ensure the legitimacy of the council's activities, the presence of a majority of orphan-nurturing female friends, con-stituting at least over half of them, is required. The father confessor of the orphanage presides over the meeting, where they first read the will of the or-phanage's founder. Then, each female friend secretly, on a separate ballot and according to her conscience, writes the name of the most deserving female friend for the office of the Mother and, folding the ballot, puts it in the ballot box, which has previously been checked in public to be empty and sealed, and which remains in the venue in front of the presiding priest. At the com-pletion of the voting process, the vote count takes place at the meeting venue, following which the names of all female friends who participated in the voting are recorded in a list based on the number of received votes. All the participants of the meeting and the presiding priest sign this list, as well as all the minutes of the voting process, and the presiding priest presents it to the [Armenian] Patriarch of Constantinople. The Patriarch, after assessing the reputation and level of trust for each female friend on the list among their colleagues and examining the virtues of each individual who received votes, within three days selects the most deserving individual from among those with the highest votes to assume the role of Mother of the orphans and overseer of the orphanage. He issues a decree to inform the members of the Society of Orphan Nurturers and the nation about his decision.

Article 13: Before assuming the office, the newly elected Mother of the orphanage, in the venue of the council of the female friends, solemnly takes an oath to be true to her title, to be the true mother of the orphans, to respect their rights, rigorously to follow the rules of the orphanage, and, with her conduct, to be a role model for everyone.

Article 14: The office of the Mother of the orphanage is the orphanage's management. She receives the Sisters who wish to become members of the congregation of Orphan Nurturers and determines their individual roles and responsibilities. She receives the orphans seeking refuge in the orphanage, chooses the appropriate individuals who will be responsible for their care and upbringing, and establishes their compensation.

Article 15: The orphanage's entire revenue and gifts are delivered to the Mother, and she is the one who authorises every necessary expenditure.

Article 16: The Mother oversees that every orphan-nurturing female friend fulfils their duties according to the rules. She admonishes the ones who do not fully perform in their roles, and after two or three admonitions, she expels those who fail to obey her from the Society.

Article 17: The Mother takes care of the orphans who found refuge there and monitors their upbringing, education, development in handicrafts, and through marriage, adoption, receiving an office or joining the ranks of the female friends of orphan nurturers, she shapes the future of each of them, endeavouring gradually to reduce the numbers of orphans in order to free spaces for the newly arrived ones.

Article 18: To facilitate the work of her office, the Mother chooses three advisers-assistants from among the female friends of orphan nurturers, and, forming with them the administrative board of the orphanage, they collectively manage all matters through mutual consultation. Besides being the Mother's advisers-assistants, these three female friends hold a special office: one of them acts as a *locum tenens* in the absence of the Mother, the second manages the bursary, and the third – the administrative office. They each hold their positions for two years; however, they can be re-elected and are free to resign from the office whenever they wish.

Article 19: At the beginning of each year, through the administrative board, the Mother reconciles the accounts of the orphanage, prepares the balance sheet for both the past and the upcoming year, and, with an explanatory statement, sends it to the Patriarch of Constantinople.

Article 20: On the basis of the order of the Patriarch regarding the balance sheet mentioned above, the Mother manages the annual expenditures of the orphanage with the condition that she attends to the orphans within the limits of the institution's revenue, and that she should be cautious not to make debts and endeavour to increase the income of the orphanage day by day.

Article 21: If, during a year, the orphanage finds itself in a position to incur additional expenses beyond the sums planned in the balance sheet, the Mother, with the decision of the administrative board, has the right to manage the same expenses, if they do not exceed the sum of 2,000 *ghurush*[215]. If they do exceed this sum, she asks, with a statement, for the Patriarch's order.

Article 22: A comprehensive list of the buildings of the orphanage and the estate property, including all assets and household goods, is registered in the general ledger. This ledger, along with the estate and official documents (*sēnēt', hēōchēt', fērman*[216] etc.), is locked in a box, and the key stays with the Mother, while the lock is sealed with the seal of the advisers.

Article 23: The orphans who have found refuge in the orphanage are brought up and educated in:

1. Armenian reading, writing, and grammar
2. Christian doctrine
3. Sacred, National, and General History
4. Arithmetic and Geometry
5. Calligraphy, drawing, and painting
6. Geography
7. General singing
8. Handicrafts

---

215 This is an Ottoman currency *kurûş*. For more details, see Cuhaj, George S. (ed.), *Standard Catalog of World Coins: 1801-1900*, 6th ed., Iola, Wi., 2009, p. 1184.
216 These were different official Ottoman certificates.

Article 24: The subjects mentioned above constitute a mandatory part of the orphans' education. The more gifted ones can also be taught a foreign language and piano, provided the orphanage's budget allows them to cover the associated expenses.

Article 25: The orphanage school is exclusively for the orphans who found refuge there, and it does not accept students from outside either for evening or daytime education.

Article 26: The officials responsible for the care and upbringing of the orphans, such as the housekeeper, cook, laundry person, maid, supervisor, instructor, teacher, and so on, are selected from among the female friends of orphan nurturers. If suitable individuals are not found internally, admission can be extended to external candidates, but on condition that young people are never admitted, and women are always given preference over men.

Here is the fruit of my ten-year achievements, which the Lord has blessed and made me worthy of imparting to the Armenian people.

I beseech God to bestow grace on me to work for my orphanage, for whose progress I have dedicated my life until my very last second. And, after my death, I ask everybody that, by keeping its current state unchanged, they zealously ensure the orphanage's enlightenment day by day.

With this testament, I particularly wish and request:

1. My orphanage should never be merged with another Armenian national institution, always remain independent, and be ruled independently according to its established rules.

2. The estates, revenues, and income of my orphanage should be preserved without loss; considerable effort should be devoted to its daily development, and by entrusting it to trustworthy Armenians, great care should be taken to ensure the future of the orphans.

3. The orphan-nurturing female friends should always manage the administration of my orphanage, and the Mother of the orphans should always be chosen from among their ranks. However, the nation should monitor the orderly provision of care by the orphanage and the zealous and accurate application of its rules. The educational and economic provisions of the orphanage only improve with time through the concord between the Society of Orphan Nurturers and the Patriarchate of Constantinople. However, the foundations should remain solid, and the principles remain unchanged.

May the Lord bless the labourers of the institution until the end of time and thwart the accomplishment of all adversities that, stemming from ill-will and imprudence, could cause the destruction of the foundations of the refuge and education centre for destitute orphans, which is by the will of God. By putting this under the protection of the Mother of God, I sign:

Abbess Srbuhi

Nshan Galfayean

12 February 1876, Thursday, on the day of Vardan's generals. [217]

We should briefly discuss this historical document. It is true that while it does not adhere to the narrow definition of a monastic rule, it serves as a significant guideline for the Sisters who have undertaken the philanthropic duty of caring for orphans. And, we may even say that it is imbued with contemporary concepts. It appears that it contains the influence of the National Constitution, which was prepared in Constantinople only 16 years earlier, and was only ratified by the sultan's government in 1863. It is evident that the membership and service of the congregation's Sisters are based on the principle of freedom. Article 7 of the "Rules of the Orphanage" stated that the Sisters of the orphanage were free to break their oath and even to forfeit the membership of the Society whenever they wished, provided that they gave at least a month's notice to the Mother of the orphanage. In the event of violations, relevant punishments were imposed, even on the Mother of the orphanage (Article 8), with decisions on this made by the patriarch (Article 11). Even though the Mother of the orphanage held her office until the end of her life, the appointment was based on electoral procedures conducted by the member-Sisters of the Galfayean congregation through a secret ballot (Article 12). The Sister, or female friend as they were also referred to, who had secured the majority of votes became the Mother of the orphanage and the congregation with the ratification from the patriarch. She then commissioned the transparent financial report of expenditures and revenues, which was annually double-checked by the administrative board and ratified by the patriarch. It is truly astounding that in this testament, among the subjects taught at the orphanage, the Armenian language, grammar, history, Christian doctrine, and so on are mentioned, but the Ottoman language (Turkish), as a taught subject, is not directly referred to anywhere. It is a salient detail that merits mention, contributing to the unique charm of this noble institution and of those devoted to its mission.

---

217 Margarean, *Kensagrut'iwn Srbuhi Mayrapeti Nshan-Galfayean*, pp. 42-52.

Dawning Hopes

In 1990, with the blessing of Garegin II, the Armenian Catholicos of the Great House of Cilicia, an affiliated community of Gayianēan Sisters was established next to the prominent orphanage of "T'rch'nots' Boyn" (Birds' Nest) in the Lebanese town of Jebeil Byblos. The wish of His Holiness was to confer on ranked and education-ready Sisters the privilege to be ordained as deaconesses, provided that the community successfully recruited new members. Regrettably, owing to a series of national-ecclesiastical changes and other adverse circumstances, and despite considerable efforts devoted to it, this initiative did not attain notable success.[218] In the 1990s, an attempt to implement a similar programme was made in the monastery of St Hrip'simē, as well as one in the 2000s in the monastery of St Gayianē. Meanwhile, a group of nuns consisting of six virgins have lived in the monastery of Ghazaravan village, located in the Aragatsotn province of the Republic of Armenia, and since since 2018. However, none of them currently holds a specific ecclesiastical rank. It is beyond the scope of the present study to provide further information about the activities of these monasteries and their nuns. However, from a canonistic point of view, the work "Nakhagits kazmut'ean ew kazmakerput'ean krōnaworuheats' kargi" (Outline of the Formation and Organisation of the Rank of Nuns) prepared for the Gayianēan community on 22-26 June 1989, in Antelias by the late Archbishop Zareh Aznaworean, a member of the congregation of the Great House of Cilicia, might be of some interest. For some reason, it was not ratified or deployed by the aforementioned Gayianēan community, and, in general, it remained unpublished. Distinguishing it from the overall research here, I would like to cite it here in its entirety: on the one hand, to preserve the work of His Grace, and on the other hand, it might prove helpful in future research avenues related to this study.

---

218 See Aznaworean, Zareh, *Hay Ekeghets'in 20-rd darun ew 21-rd daru shemin* (Armenian Church in the 20th Century and at the Threshold of the 21st Century), Nicosia, 2005, pp. 87-92.

OUTLINE OF THE FORMATION AND ORGANISATION OF THE RANK OF NUNS
(Only the situation of adults has been considered below)

STATUTORY POINTS

I. NAME, AFFILIATION, AND SUBORDINATION

1. The Order of Nuns, which was founded by the mercy of God in the year 1990 of the Saviour, bears the name of Gayianē, one of the female apostles[219] who effected the conversion of the entire Armenia, and is called "Srbuhi Gayianēi miabanut'iwn" (Congregation of Holy Gayianē) or simply "Gayianēan k'uyreri miabanut'iwn" (Congregation of Gayianēan Sisters).

2. The Congregation of Gayianēan Sisters belongs to the Catholicosate of the Great House of Cilicia and is entirely under its auspices.

3. The first temporary centre for the nuns is the T'ṛch'nots' Boyn institution in Jebeil, which belongs to the Catholicosate of the Great House of Cilicia.

4. The Order of Nuns is an independent congregation, whose head and director is a Mother Superior elected by the congregation. However, in spiritual and administrative questions, the congregation is subordinate and accountable directly to the Catholicos of the Great House of Cilicia.

5. The congregation is governed by this statute, which is implemented (and, if reformed, will be implemented) after its ratification by the Catholicos of the Great House of Cilicia.

II. DEFINITION OF MISSION

6. The monastic life of the Order of Nuns is not its ultimate goal per se, nor is it solely living a life of self-reflection. By dedicating themselves to the service of God, the Armenian Apostolic Church, and the Armenian people, the sisters included here share a common goal and mission:

a) To lead a pure and irreproachable life, embodying, to the best of their abilities, the God-pleasing virtues of active Christian faith, unwavering hope, and selfless love, and with it to serve as a model and to weave the glory of God with deeds, following the commandment of our Lord Jesus Christ: "Let your light shine before others, so that they may see your good works and give glory to your Father in heaven" (Mt 5:16).

b) To dedicate themselves to philanthropy, considering the care and solicitude for orphans, widows, the poor, the homeless, the sick, and the disabled as their primary responsibility because "Religion that is pure and undefiled before God, the Father, is this: to care for orphans and widows in their distress, and to keep oneself unstained by the world" (Jas 1:27).

---

219 On the tradition of female apostles in the Armenian tradition, see Zakarian, *Women, Too, Were Blessed*, pp. 71-72, 76-78, 83, 98-99.

c) To engage in educational activities, providing instruction and teaching, especially to those children in our nation who are deprived of this opportunity owing to their social and family circumstances.

d) To preach Christ's Holy Gospel with their words and deeds, without compulsion and constraint, "whether the time is favourable or unfavourable" (2 Tim 4:2).

e) To remain devoted to the confession of faith of the Armenian Apostolic Church and the sacred traditions of the nation and, with the glee of the new days, to bequeath and propagate them in their milieu.

III. ADMISSION AND GENERAL PRINCIPLES

7. The Order of Nuns admits all those young ladies and widows who have an inclination towards monastic life and a willingness to dedicate themselves to the apostolic work.

8. Individuals who become members of the Congregation of Gayianēan Sisters are referred to as *Sisters*. They lead a communal life under the leadership of the great lady, who is called *Mother*, and absolutely everyone is expected to obey her.

9. The Sisters live, pray, and work together, and carry out their individual duties without complaint, with love and obedience.

10. The Sisters serve unconditionally, without a salary or any expectations.

IV. APPLICATION FORM AND CONDITIONS

11. An applicant to the Congregation of Gayianēan Sisters must be 16 years of age.

12. She must be in good health to withstand the difficulties of monastic life and endure the hard labour that is part of her mission.

13. She must provide, in writing (orally, in exceptional circumstances), detailed information about her background, education, family and friends, occupation, and mainly the reasons for applying for monastic life.

14. From the beginning and without preconditions, she must commit to hard labour and complete obedience.

V. ACCEPTANCE AND PROBATION PERIOD

15. After meeting the preliminary requirements, the individual is temporarily admitted as a teacher or worker to the "T'ṛch'nots' Boyn" or any other institution under the auspices of the Monastic Order, depending on their level and preparedness.

16. After being admitted but before the novitiate, the individual must *pass the probation and ministry period*.

17. The probation period must be at least two years. Only in exceptional cases can this period be reduced, considering the applicant's age, spiritual maturity, and cultivation.

18. If, after the mentioned two-year probation period, the applicant turns out not to be suitable for a monastic life, the application is rejected. Only rarely can the probation period last up to four years.

VI. NOVITIATE

19. After the two-year probation period, if the individual is deemed suitable, she is admitted as a novice.

20. The novitiate also lasts at least two years and, if necessary, longer, considering the progress made by the individual.

21. From the day the individual is admitted as a novice, she wears the special clothing of the Monastic Order without being considered a nun – meaning, she has not yet taken the vow of monastic life.

22. The novitiate differs from the probation period in that the individual begins to dedicate herself more seriously to monastic life and mission preparation, displaying more fondness towards praying, increased efforts in education, and heightened spiritual motivation.

VII. PREPARATION

23. Both the probation period and the novitiate are considered *preparation periods*, which, in addition to ministry, include the following:

a) *Study Courses* (scheduled one day a week, these courses include the following subjects: Introduction to the Holy Book, Classical Armenian for Beginners, Ancient and Modern Armenian Literature, History of the Armenian Church, Ethics, and so on)

b) *Religious-Ritualistic Knowledge* (foundations of Christian faith, introduction to the canonical hours, study of the *sharakans*)

c) *Immersion in the Spiritual Life* (life of prayer, spiritual consultation one hour per week and one hour of learning the Holy Book, preferably on Saturday evening)

d) *Knowledge about the Mission* (practical aspects of social service, basic pedagogical knowledge, first aid, and so on)

VIII. MONASTIC LIFE AND MONASTIC VOWS

24. After the completion of the novitiate, if it is determined that the novice is suitable for monastic life, she takes special vows appropriate to monastic life before the Holy Altar and, with a special consecration ceremony and blessing, receives the monastic veil.

25. The monastic vows are *Obedience, Poverty, Renunciation,* and *Ministry.*

i. The first vow is *obedience*, which the nun pledges to her Creator and the Lord of the Souls, the Father Saviour of All, as well as to her soul's earthly leader – Mother Superior.

Voluntary obedience is an actual expression of true filiation and filial love. It is like when a Christian becomes the true child of the heavenly Father and becomes worthy of the grace to be called a brother, sister, or mother of our Lord and Holy Saviour Jesus Christ, as He, the Lord, revealed himself: "For whoever does the will of my Father in heaven is my brother and sister and mother" (Mt 12:50). And Christ himself became the first example of complete obedience effected by filial love, as the Apostle says: "Let the same mind be in you that was in Christ Jesus, who [...] humbled himself and became obedient to the point of death – even death on a cross" (Phil 2:5, 8).

Voluntary obedience is also the most genuine expression of Christ-like virtues of gentleness and humility, with which the nun searches and finds the absolute serenity of her soul, as Christ himself taught, saying: "Take my yoke upon you, and learn from me; for I am gentle and humble in heart, and you will find rest for your souls" (Mt 11:29). And as the obedience pledged to God is complete, characterised by unconditional love and absolute trust, so should the obedience pledged to Mother Superior be also complete, tied with love and sealed with the seal of trust.

ii. The second vow is *poverty*, when the nun pledges to abandon the earthly treasures voluntarily in order to please God.

Voluntary poverty is the first step to liberating one's soul. With it, the nun endeavours to drive away everything that can become an obstacle for her soul, tie her down to the world, condition and bind her to the world, and render fruitless her life, good wishes and disposition, hard labour, virtuous vigilance, and efforts to reach perfection. For our Saviour Christ reminds us that those who do not abandon worldly goods and riches resemble the land covered in thorns, in which the fallen grains of His words are doomed to infertility: "And others are those sown among the thorns: these are the ones who hear the word, but the cares of the world, and the lure of wealth, and the desire for other things come in and choke the word, and it yields nothing" (Mk 4:18-19). Meanwhile, in the nun's soul, the Heavenly Teacher's words continuously resonate: "For what will it profit them if they gain the whole world but forfeit their life?" (Mt 16:26).

Indeed, the first example of voluntary poverty was offered by Christ himself to his own. Not only did He strip himself of the opulence of divine glory and put on the dress of a servant (Phil 2:6-7), but He also lived on the earth in voluntary poverty (cf. Lk 9:3), and it was to the poor that He gave His first blessing: "Blessed are you who are poor, for yours is the kingdom of God" (Lk 6:20). At the same time, He taught His followers that voluntary poverty was the perfect means to dedicate oneself to God, as He told the rich young man: "If you want to be good,[220] go, sell what you own, and give the money to the poor, and you will have treasure in heaven; then come, follow me" (Mk 10:21-22).

Voluntary poverty is a wise choice made by the nun on her path to acquiring true and eternal wealth, as she sees her only treasure in God: she, therefore, sells what she owns to come into possession of the "fine pearl" (Mt 13:45-46), and God rewards her for her losses a hundredfold, as Jesus promised his followers, saying: "Truly I tell you, there is no one who has left house or brothers or sisters or mother or father or children or fields, for my sake and for the sake of the good news, who will not receive a hundredfold now in this age – houses, brothers and sisters, mothers and children, and fields, with persecutions – and in the age to come eternal life" (Mk 10:29-30).

Voluntary poverty is also a true means of Christ's missionary path to dedicating oneself to serving others; an example of it was, once again, set by our Lord Himself. Truly, Apostle Paul, the herald of divine truth, pro-claims: "For you know the generous act of our Lord Jesus Christ, that though he was rich, yet for your sakes he became poor, so that by his pov-erty you might become rich" (2 Cor 8:9). The nun who follows in Christ's footsteps commits to voluntary poverty so that, after relieving herself of the burden of material goods and worldly riches and enriching herself with spiritual blessings, she can also enrich the lives of others by gener-ously sharing the same gifts and spiritual blessings. And similar to Christ himself, who always voluntarily offered succour to the destitute, despite His poverty on earth (Jn 12:5, 13:29), the nun, from the savings acquired through abstention from indulgence, offers succour to an orphan and widow, the poor and the deprived, by enriching their lives with her pov-erty. As the Apostle, filled with the mind of Christ, states through the ex-perience of his own life of voluntary poverty: "We are treated as impos-tors, and [...] as sorrowful, yet always rejoicing; as poor, yet making many rich; as having nothing, and yet possessing everything" (2 Cor 6:8, 10).

iii.   The third vow is the *renunciation of the world*, which is the nun's promise to dedicate her entire self to God "for the sake of the kingdom of heaven" (Mt 19:12). Renunciation of the world is, first of all, the renunciation of "earthly mentality and lifestyle," which is characterised by the dishar-mony of reasoning and will, wishes and disposition, words and deeds, as

---

220 This clause is not found in the English Bible.

well as by disorder, feebleness, and lack of restraint. The nun, as an em-
bodiment of a faithful Christian, adopts an organised, harmonious, wise,
orderly, moderate, and prudent lifestyle in everything in order to become
renewed in the spirit and reformed in mentality, "with the new self, created according to the likeness of God" wishing to live "in true righteous-
ness and holiness" (Eph 4:24).

Renunciation of the world, which in itself entails relinquishing earthly
engagements and concerns, means dedication to God's work. The nun,
compelled to propagate God's kingdom, fruitfully cultivate love, and fer-
vently engage in "the work of the Lord", commits to renouncing the
sweetness of marital life and, without the demands and ties of familial and
social life, makes the work of God the only object of her concern; just like
the blessed Apostle Paul points out: "And the unmarried woman and the
virgin are anxious about the affairs of the Lord, so that they may be holy
in body and spirit; but the married woman is anxious about the affairs of
the world, how to please her husband" (1 Cor 7:34).

Even though this life of complete perseverance, spiritual vigilance,
self-restraint, and self-control is arduous; nevertheless, it is lived with the
help of God's exclusive graces, and, for this, it becomes a life of grace for
the one who accepts it.

iv.   The fourth and final vow is *ministry*, which is simultaneously the combi-
nation of, and complementarity to, all the other vows. Among the monastic virtues, the most practical and significant one is diligence, which
does not permit the poisonous rust of laziness to corrode the mind and
soul of the nun and to make her the victim of the errors of deadly indo-
lence such as detrimental interests, irrational worries, immodest and inappropriate conversations, and so on, as pointed out by the Apostle (1
Tm 5:13). Therefore, the nun, like an industrious bee, dedicates herself to
work, ministry, and charity, always listening to the apostolic voice which
says, "do not be weary in doing what is right" (2 Thes 3:13).

Truly, "just as the body without the spirit is dead" and "faith without
works is also dead" (Jas 2:26), so, without active service, obedience, poverty, and renunciation of the world are devoid of meaning and dead. This
is why it is the second most significant side of a monastic calling, next to
the life of prayer, and even more prioritised, like the blessed translator,
vardapet Eznik Koghbats'i, says in his advice to monks: "The best monk
is one who, with prayers, extends his hands towards God; however, even
more important is the one who attends to the needs of his brothers."[221]

---

221 Eznik Koghbats'i, *Eghts Aghandots'* (Against the Sects), Yerevan, 1994, pp. 256-
257.

Ministry, not negotiated, meant, without exception, for everyone in need, the deprived, and the fallen; service without complaint, with perfect love and joy, philanthropy, and zealousness, remembering the immense and irreplaceable value of each human being in the eyes of God and respecting everybody's individuality and dignity – such voluntary service is the sole treasure with which a nun feels herself wealthy, and by consistently engaging in it, she enriches herself for an extended period. Because the one who serves voluntarily is rewarded manifold: first, in the present, bringing her joy and causing her to flourish with grace, about which the great *vardapet* Eznik Koghbats'i says: "Whatever grace God bestows on you, employ them for the needs of the ones in need so that the grace will overflow like a water spring and you be glorified."[222] And, second, there will be the greatest and eternal reward: who serves in the name of God's love accumulates treasure with God, as the wise author of the *Proverbs* says: "Whoever is kind to the poor lends to the Lord, and will be repaid in full" (Prv 19:17). And if Christ says that "a cup of cold water" given to the "little ones" of this world will not go unrewarded (Mt 10:42), then it is just that an individual who has dedicated herself to this service hoped to hear, on the day, the following happy call from the lips of the Just Judge: "Come, you that are blessed by my Father, inherit the kingdom prepared for you from the foundation of the world; for I was hungry and you gave me food, I was thirsty and you gave me something to drink, I was a stranger and you welcomed me, I was naked and you gave me clothing, I was sick and you took care of me, I was in prison and you visited me. [...] Truly I tell you, just as you did it to one of the least of these who are members of my family, you did it to me" (Mt 25:34-36, 40).

IX. DEFINITION AND RENEWAL OF VOWS

26. The monastic vows mentioned above are temporary, for a period of three years. Every Sister may renew her vows or not. Those who do not wish to renew their vows, one month before the end of the term, inform Mother Superior about it and part from the community with dignity and blessing. In the future, these Sisters can again join the Monastic Order if their readmission is deemed appropriate and beneficial. And those who leave the Order without waiting for the end of the term and without receiving special permission are deemed expelled and cannot return.

---

222 Ibid., pp. 244-245

X. DEACONESSES

27. There must be several deaconesses among the nuns of the community who, on a daily basis during the service, will sing exhortative sermons, do the censing, and read the Gospel, as these duties cannot be performed by nuns who do not hold the rank of deacon.

28. There are no differences between deaconesses and other nuns in the monastic life. They only differ in dress, for deaconesses wear a cross on the veil at the forehead and a stole hanging on the right side of the belt.

XI. LIFESTYLE

29. The main principle of monastic life is "Prayers and Work". One of our blessed fathers, translator Eznik Koghbats'i, in his directives addressed to monks, summarises the main three points of their life as follows: "Obey with love! Pray with hope! Work with faith, and during the heavenly wedding you shall be illuminated!"[223]

30. Personal and communal prayer must be the essential element and necessary sustenance of everyone's life. Every morning and evening, nuns must participate in the services according to the canonical service of the Armenian Church. The canonical service is led by the Mother Superior, the vicar, or one of the senior Sisters, following appointment.

31. Once a week, every Sunday, the Divine Liturgy is served in the institution's chapel, and all Sisters partake in the Holy Communion of the Saviour's Holy Flesh and Blood.

32. All Sisters live together and in unity, adhering to the principle of equality in an environment of love, harmony, and mutual respect.

33. At the foundations of relationships, there must be respect and reverence. In particular, the younger ones must be entirely respectful towards those who are older than them.

34. Within the institution, Sisters receive shelter, food, clothing, and medical care, whereas in old age or during sickness, they receive special care.

35. They dine together at designated hours. When late due to sickness or other reasons, arrangements must only be made by the Sister responsible for the catering.

36. Inside the institution, every Sister is required to assume the role or responsibility of a cleaner, caterer, housekeeper, cook, nurse, instructor, teacher, laundry attendant, manager of orphans, and so on, and she must perform her duties without complaint, with joy, and honour. At the discretion of the Mother Superior, any of them may take on a role or responsibility outside the institution.

---

223 Ibid., pp. 244-245.

37. Roles are assigned based on ability and necessity. There are no roles considered more reputable or low. The most essential thing is to fulfil the role faultlessly.

38. For fulfilling their roles, Sisters should not expect to receive appreciation. The only genuine appreciation for a task executed with excellence should be personal satisfaction. And after its execution, they should recall Christ's words, "when you have done all that you were ordered to do, say, 'We are worthless slaves; we have done only what we ought to have done!'" (Lk 17:10).

39. Besides daily chores, Sisters should pay special attention to their spiritual growth and edification, and, to that end, they should frequently read from the books provided and assigned.

40. Sisters can address personal or group questions regarding spiritual life and matters of faith to the priest appointed by the Catholicos of the Great House of Cilicia, who, in the role of the Father Confessor and spiritual adviser, visits the institution once a week.

41. At least once a week, everybody should assemble to discuss issues concerning different aspects of their life and mission or have a spiritual conversation on any other matter.

42. To go on a visit or to participate in a public event outside of the institution, every Sister must have the permission of the Mother Superior.

43. The institution covers all incurred expenses, whether personal or related to duties.

44. If needed, Sisters must inform the Mother Superior or her deputy in writing about any difficulties or complaints they have.

XII. Mother Superior

45. The Mother Superior is elected by the members of the order for a five-year term. She can be re-elected by the will of Sisters after the end of her term.

46. The election takes place at the general council of sisters, which is convened once in five years (with some exceptions) and is presided over by a priest adviser appointed by His Holiness Catholicos of the Great House of Cilicia. The election is conducted by a secret ballot and requires a two-thirds majority. In the event of a simple majority, the names of those who received most of the votes are presented to His Holiness the Catholicos: within three days, he selects the most suitable candidate from among the worthy ones and announces his choice by the official decree of the Catholicos.

47. Before commencing her tenure, the Mother Superior takes solemn vows to adhere obediently to the order and canons of the Armenian Apostolic Church, to the Catholicos of the Great House of Cilicia and his executive decisions, to the monastic rule of the nunnery, as well as to being a true Mother for her fellow nuns, respecting and protecting their rights and, with her deeds, serving as a positive role model for them.

48. On the Sunday after the elections, the newly elected Mother Superior receives a special order of blessing in front of the holy bema of the church from a high-ranking clergy appointed by His Holiness the Catholicos of the Great House of Cilicia.

49. If the Mother Superior cannot perform her duties owing to a serious illness, the management of affairs passes to the Governing Body. In the event of an incurable illness, if it is not feasible to convene a general council of Sisters immediately, the Sisters in the central administration choose a deputy from among the members of the Governing Body so that she will assume the responsibilities of the Mother Superior until the next general council.

50. In the event of the Mother Superior's sudden death, until the new elections, the Governing Body deals with the affairs and management if a prompt organisation of the general council is not impossible. If a prompt organisation of the general council is impossible, during a period of three days after the burial, Sisters in the central administration, with the chairmanship of the priest adviser appointed by His Holiness, select a deputy who will assume the management until the general council.

51. Whoever slanders the Mother Superior is severely punished; depending on the seriousness of the matter, they may even be expelled from the order. However, if it appears that the Mother Superior has not remained faithful to her office and title and, through her behaviour and actions, has caused moral or material damage to the order and institution, she is subject to just accusations. The accusations are sent to His Holiness the Catholicos through the priest adviser appointed by him. If they are proven, His Holiness the Catholicos himself admonishes her and calls her to rectify her conduct, depending on the nature of the accusations. And if the Mother Superior fails to comply and continues in the same way, then she is removed from her office and, if appropriate, is announced as defrocked.

XIII. RESPONSIBILITIES OF THE MOTHER SUPERIOR

52. The Mother Superior is the head of the nuns and, at the same time, the supervisor of the "T'r̄ch'nots' Boyn" institution. In constant consultation with the Governing Body, her primary responsibilities are:

    i. to receive applications for the convent.

    ii. to determine each Sister's role and allocate responsibilities.

    iii. like a thoughtful mother, to monitor the life of the nuns and to ensure the fulfilment of their roles and responsibilities, making necessary arrangements and remarks with a generous spirit for the benefit of the given individual, the community, and the institution.

    iv. like a devout custodian for her believing Sisters, "to be an example of humbleness and humility, righteousness and truth, vigilance and tears, peace and serenity, love and patience, law and justice, labour and perseverance, decency and sobriety, chastity and purity, discipline, prayer, and fasting," as defined by the second Illuminator of our faith, the thrice-blessed great patriarch Saint Grigor.[224]

v.   to ensure order and harmony within the internal monastic life; to create favourable conditions and means for life, labour, and the accomplishment of one's mission.

vi.   to admonish and instruct Sisters who have been accused of poor discipline, disobedience, and other offences; to punish those who will not heed her, guiding them zealously on the path of justice and truth, with the aim of presenting them to God in an immaculate and perfect state.

vii.   to attend to current affairs and make requisite arrangements for them.

viii.   to admit staff required in the institution and assign their duties and salaries.

ix.   after examination, to admit those orphans and the destitute of our nation who are eligible to find refuge in the institution.

x.   to monitor the education and upbringing of the sheltered children and youth, as well as their extracurricular activities and development.

xi.   to oversee the property and income of the institution; to determine the requisite expenses and zealously monitor the institution's finances.

xii.   to endeavour to secure new sources of income and, to the best of her abilities, to ensure the self-sufficiency and prosperity of the institution and the community.

xiii.   at the start of each year, to prepare an overall report of all the expenditure and income of the institution and the community, as well as the revenue budget for the upcoming year, and send it to the Catholicos of the Great House of Cilicia along with an explanatory statement.

xiv.   for any exceptionally big expenses outside the revenue budget, special permission should be requested from His Holiness the Catholicos.

xv.   at the end of the tenure, before the general council of the community, an overall report detailing the activities and accounts should be prepared to be presented before the general council for examination.

xvi.   approximately six months before convening the general council, its date should be announced and an invitation sent, especially to those sisters who work outside the institution.

---

224 See *Srboy Hōrn Meroy Eranelwoyn Grigori Lusaworch'i Yachakhapatum Chaṛk'* (Dogmatical Speeches of Our Holy Father the Blessed Gregory the Illuminator), Ējmiatsin, 1894, p. 260.

XIV. GOVERNING BODY

53. To manage the affairs of the institution and community, the Mother Superior has an adviser and three assistant Sisters, who form the Governing Body with her.

54. Only Sisters who have at least five years of community life experience can be elected as members of the Governing Body.

55. Sisters are elected to the Governing Body by the General Council once in five years. In the event of a member's long-term illness or sudden death, with the approval of the Sisters of the central administration, a new Sister is appointed to the same role.

56. The Sisters, members of the Governing Body, are the Mother Superior's advisers and assistants, while at the same time, each of them has her own special position.

    i.   The first holds the position of the *deputy Mother Superior*, both during the latter's presence and absence from the establishment.

    ii. The second holds the position of the *secretary*: she keeps records of all the decisions and practical orders.

    iii. The third is the *treasurer* and *accountant* responsible for all material transactions of the institution.

57. The responsibilities of the Governing Body led by the Mother Superior are defined in this last section pertaining to the responsibilities (see Article 52, points i-xvi).

XV. GENERAL COUNCIL

58. The General Council is the highest legislative assembly of the community of nuns, which is convened once every five years with the participation of all members of the Community of Gayianēan Sisters. If required, as in the event of the Mother Superior's death, a special session of the General Council convenes.

59. The General Council is summoned by the Mother Superior (and, in the event of her death, by the Governing Body), who must announce it approximately six months before the meeting, and the sisters who work outside the community must be informed about the date of the meeting at least three months before it is convened.

60. The General Council convenes behind closed doors and is presided over by the Mother Superior. In the event of the Mother Superior's passing away, a cleric appointed by the Catholicos of the Great House of Cilicia presides over the council.

61. The General Council has its secretary, who is elected at the opening of the meeting and dismissed at the meeting's final session after the recitation and ratification of the records of the final session.

62. The responsibilities of the General Council are:
    i.   to examine and evaluate the report of the activities of the Mother Superior and the Governing Body.
    ii. on the basis of the report, to analyse the reasons behind the recorded successes and failures of the community's general activities; through constructive criticism, to eliminate the factors that contributed to failures and to underscore or develop factors which may contribute to success, and with this to determine a new route to be adopted in the coming five years.
    iii. to elect the new Mother Superior.
    iv. from among the community members to choose three Sisters for the Governing Body.

XVI. DISCIPLINARY REGULATIONS

63. Any disobedient Sister who breaks the general rules of the institution or the Order, if she does not reform after being admonished two or three times and advised to reconsider her actions and continues to behave in the same way, will be expelled from the order by the decision of the Mother Superior and her advisers.

***

The "Outline of the Formation and Organisation of the Rank of Nuns" prepared by His Grace of the blessed memory may be appropriate for a strict monastic environment. However, even with all its valuable aspects, it is difficult to imagine how some of the canons would be implemented in practice today, even in the church environment. Setting aside the first part of the "Monastic Rule", which reflects a medieval worldview, it is necessary to evaluate the non-permanent nature of the monastic vows (Article 26), that is, a nun was not required to renew her vows after the period of three years and would be released with a blessing from the monastic order. The regulations related to the work of the council and the election system are of great importance; in the case of violations – the penalties were imposed not only on the ordinary members of the community but also on the Mother Superior if the accusations brought against her were justified. This monastic rule has some similarities with the canons of the Galfayean orphanage. However, in comparison with the latter, this one has a noteworthy advantage, which is its section X with articles 27 and 28 dedicated to deaconesses. His Grace Archbishop Zareh, who was undoubtedly one of the most prominent theologians, exegetes, translators, specialists of *sharakan*s, and church musicians of the Armenian Apostolic Church of our time, was well-informed about the tradition of the rank of deaconesses in our church. He was an advocate for its preservation when he defined the necessity to ordain them within the Gayianēan Monastic Order, so that the deaconesses would acquire authority through a religious bestowal and "on a daily basis during the service, will sing exhortative sermons, do the censing, and read the Gospel, as these duties cannot be performed by nuns who do not hold the rank of deacon" (Article 27).

Several additional historical factors are also worth mentioning here, for they demonstrate that in the Armenian Church, the church activities of deaconesses were not necessarily linked to monastic communities, despite the earlier mentioned nuns from the nunneries of St Katarinē of New Julfa, St Stepʻanos of Tbilisi, Galfayean orphanage of Constantinople, and the Gayianēan Monastic Order of the "Tʻṛchʻnotsʻ Boyn". There were also deaconesses involved in the simple pastoral service or the activities of certain parishes. Within this context, deaconesses Anna and Hṛipʻsimē Mnatsʻakanean should be mentioned, as the inscriptions embroidered with golden thread on their stoles testify to them being in pastoral service at the diocesan cathedral of Astrakhan in Russia. Here are these inscriptions:

> This stole was given as a memorial to Anna Mnatsʻakanean Getʻsemanentsʻ for the soul of her late sister. Of Anna, female deacon, at the door of the Cathedral of the Holy Mother of God in Astrakhan, 6 September 1837.

This stole is a memorial for the soul of Hṛipʻsimē Mnatsʻakanean / A female deacon in the Cathedral of the Holy Mother of God in Astrakhan, 1837.[225]

---

225 See Figure: Յիշատակ եւ ուրարս Աննայ Մնացականեան Գեթսեմանենց վասն հոգւոյ հանգուցեալ քեռն իւրոյ: Աննայի կուսան սարկաւագի ի դուռն սրբոյ Աստուածածնի Տաճարին յԱստրախան 6.9.1837:
Յիշատակ է ուրարս վասն Հոգւոյ Հռիփսիմէ Մնացականեան: Կուսան սարկաւագին ի Սբ. Աստուածածնի Տաճարին որ յԱստրախան 1837.

Stole embroidered with silver and golden thread. Inscription at the top: "Jesus Christ, St Stephen, St Peter." At the bottom: "This stole is a memorial for the soul of Hṛip'simē Mnats'akanean / A female deacon in the Cathedral of the Holy Mother of God in Astrakhan, 1837", Ējmiatsin, Treasury.

Stole embroidered with silver and golden thread. At the top, on the left – Apostle Peter; on the right – Jesus Christ; at the bottom, St Stephen, the first deacon, with the censer and the incense box in his hands. Inscription: "This stole was given as a memorial to Anna Mnats'akanean Get'semanents' for the soul of her late sister / Of Anna, female deacon, at the door of the Cathedral of the Holy Mother of God in Astrakhan, 6 September 1837", Ējmiatsin, Treasury.

This pair of stoles belonged to two sisters, hailing from Yerevan, who lived in the town of Astrakhan and served as deaconesses in the local church of the Holy Mother of God.

A short time later, in 1842, deaconesses Eghisabēt' and Katarinē Sarbashean, again from Astrakhan, appealed to the Synod of Ējmiatsin with a request to permit them to participate in pastoral services in accordance with the rank of deacon, and following the example of the deaconesses of Tbilisi, to visit the houses of prominent Armenians during funerals and church feasts.[226]

> With great respect, we earnestly entreat you, Illuminating Synod, with this [letter] to consider taking care of us and to grant us permission to serve in accordance with our calling, and we enquire whether, during the feast of Easter and house blessings when we visit the homes of prominent people in our nation, we may read the Gospel, sing songs and *sharakan*s, similar to the priests, as is the customary practice, or to read the Gospel during the liturgy in the town's church without a problem and to recite psalms upon the esteemed deceased women and young ladies.[227]

The letter of response of the Synod of Ējmiatsin to this request has also reached us.[228] According to it, the petitioning deaconesses were permitted to perform ritualistic ceremonies within the Armenian community of Astrakhan.[229]

---

226 Republic of Armenia, National Archives, section 56, list 1, work 3045. See also Mkrtch'yan, "Sarkavaguhineri tsaṛayut'yunn u pashtonĕ Hay Aṛak'elakan Ekeghets'um", p. 44.

227 Republic of Armenia, National Archives, section 56, list 1, work 3045. See also Mkrtch'yan, "Sarkavaguhineri tsaṛayut'yunn u pashtonĕ Hay Aṛak'elakan Ekeghets'um", p. 44: Մեծաւ պատկառանօք վստահութիւն կալաք թախանձել սովաւ ի Լուսաւորչական Սինհոդուէդ զի բարեհաճեսցի իմամ տանել մեզ եւ շնորհել զբացարձակ կանոն կատարելոյ զպաշտամունս՝ պատշաճաւորս աստիճանի եւ կոչման մերոյ եւ միանգամայն հրամայել թէ կարե՞մք արդեօք ի տօնի Զատկի եւ Ջրօրհնեաց ի տունս երեւելեաց ազգի մերոյ՝ յորս շրջիմք ըստ սովորութեան՝ ընթեռնուլ զԱւետարան, եւ երգել զերգս եւ զշարականս՝ գոր երգեն ըստ պատշաճի աւուր քահանայք կամ յեկեղեցիս քաղաքիս ընթեռնուլ զԱւետարան ի ժամ պատարագի անարգel՝ նոյնպէս հնա՞ր իցէ մեզ սաղմոս կարդալ երբեմն ի վերայ պատուաւոր կանանց եւ օրիորդաց ննջեցելոց:

228 Republic of Armenia, National Archives, section 56, list 1, work 3045.

229 See Mkrtch'yan, "Sarkavaguhineri tsaṛayut'yunn u pashtonĕ Hay Aṛak'elakan Ekeghets'um", p. 45.

Additionally, the name of Archdeaconess Nazeni Kēōzumean was associated with the settlement of Sēōlēōz (Sölöz) of Bursa region, which had a siz-
able Armenian population, and where in the 1830s, along with the priest Ni-
koghayos, she was ordained as deaconess by Patriarch Stepʻanos Aghawni.[230]

The last deaconess of the Armenian Church[231] was the late Hṛipʻsimē
Sasunean[232] from among the Sisters of the Galfayean community of Constantinople, who passed away in 2007. When it seemed that with the death of deaconess sister Hṛipʻsimē Sasunean, the golden thread of the Armenian Church
tradition of deaconesses was forever severed, providence caused a fortunate
event: on 24 September 2017, in the Prelacy of Tehran of the Great House of
Cilicia, Archbishop Sebouh Sarkissian performed an ordination ceremony of
a new deaconess. The newly ordained deaconess was Ani-Kristi Manvelian[233],

---

230 See Abraham Ayvazean, *Shar Hay Kensagrutʻeantsʻ* (A Series of Armenian Biog-
     raphies), Constantinople, 1893, p. 109; see also Abraham Ayvazean, "Awag sarka-
     waguhi mĕ i Sēōlēōz" (An Archdeaconess from Sēōlēōz), *Hay Khōsnak*, 5-6, 1933,
     p. 82.

231 Another Sister of the Galfayean community was subdeaconess Gayiane
     Tulkʻatĕrean, whose dedication took place on 21 November 2006 in Constanti-
     nople. On the same day, she received the four ranks of the office of *dpir* and the
     veil. On 17 March 2007, during the Sunday eve ceremony, she decided to take her
     vows, and twenty days later, on 7 April 2007, during the sermon of the liturgy of
     the Holy Easter, she was pronounced "Sister Gayiane" as a member of the
     Galfayean congregation's community. On 19 November 2011, she received the
     right to wear a stole; on 21 November 2011, she read out the Holy Gospel from
     Luke 11:14-23 for the first time. Sister Gayiane was ordained as subdeaconess on
     23 November 2014 by Bishop Sahak Mashalean in Constantinople. Here, I would
     like to thank Mr Ishkhan Chiftʻchean for bringing this information to my atten-
     tion.

232 Deaconess Hṛipʻsimē Sasunean was ordained in 1982 by His Grace Patriarch of
     Constantinople, Archbishop Shnorhkʻ Galustean. In 1990, with the latter's
     knowledge and the invitation of Garegin II Catholicos of the Great House of Ci-
     licia, she arrived in Lebanon and was appointed as the headmistress of the Arme-
     nian orphanage of "Tʻṛchʻnotsʻ Boyn" in Jebeil. The plan of His Grace was that
     this reverend deaconess, with her experience, would contribute to the success of
     the newly established Gayianēan monastic order, finding new candidates for the
     nuns of this community. On 2 June 1991, in Mother Church of Antelias, the first
     ceremony of the bestowal of the veil of celibacy of sister Kʻnarik Gaypʻakʻean took
     place (see Ghewond Chʻēpēyean, "Sarkavaguhinerĕ Hayotsʻ Ekeghetsʻu mēj"
     (Deaconesses in the Armenian Church), *Hask* 4-5, 1989, pp. 169-171; p. 170).

233 See Hratch Tchilingirian, "Historic Ordination: Tehran Prelacy of the Armenian
     Church Ordains Deaconess", *The Armenian Weekly*, 16 January 2018,

who was ordained not for the closed environment of an abbacy but to contribute to the pastoral service of the Diocese. Her activities were not limited to a monastic environment but were intended for pastoral service among the community and for the benefit of the people. In this respect, the speech of the Primate deserves commendation, for he has stated the following:

> Today, our Church is confronting the imperative of self-examination and self-critique. It is imperative to rejuvenate the participation of the people in the social, educational, and service spheres of the Church. It is our deep conviction that the active participation of women in the life of our Church would allow Armenian women to be involved more enthusiastically and vigorously, and would allow them to be connected and engaged. They would provide dedicated and loving service [to the people]. The deaconess, no doubt, would also be a spiritual and church-dedicated mother, educator, and why not, a model woman through her example. It is with this deep conviction that we are performing this ordination, with the hope that we are neither the first nor the last to do it.[234]

Dr Hratch Tchilingirian's discussion of this rare event of ordination in our time in his article "Historic Ordination: Tehran Prelacy of the Armenian Church Ordains Deaconess," is also of great interest. In addition, a noteworthy incident from a reliable source has been brought to my attention, which I will describe below:

> On 29 December 2002, the Prelate of the Armenian Diocese of Argentina, Archbishop Gisak Muratean, on the occasion of the feast of St Stephen the protodeacon and protomartyr, ordained Maria Carmen Ozkul as deaconess alongside three other male deacons in the cathedral of St Gregory the Illuminator of Buenos Aires. After that, he ordained Mara Fetichino K'eorōghlean as deaconess to serve in the Armenian church of Cordoba. Unfortunately, His Grace Gisak was soon subjected to "strong pressure from Ējmiatsin". Even though it is within the jurisdiction of the Prelate to perform such ordinations for the needs of his prelacy, Ējmiatsin, notwithstanding, demanded that His Grace immediately depose the deaconesses he had ordained. He informed the reliable source mentioned above about this during their meeting in Buenos Aires (18 June 2019). When His Grace Gisak refused to depose the

---

<https://armenianweekly.com/2018/01/16/historic-ordination-tehran-diocese-armenian-church-ordains-deaconess/>, accessed on 16 January 2024.

234 Ibid. See also S. Galachean, "Hay Ekeghets'woy sarkawaguhinerĕ erēk ew aysōr" (The Deaconesses of the Armenian Church, Yesterday and Today), *Zhamanak Daily*, December 23, 2017, p. 3.

deaconesses, the argument led to Ējmiatsin threatening to suspend the Archbishop himself. Finally, the issue "was resolved" by completely banning the deaconesses from ascending to the altar and serving during the liturgy. In any case, this created an unpleasant and undesirable atmosphere. One of the deaconesses, feeling offended, has stopped attending the church, while the other one continues to serve in Cordoba by joining the choir's singing and assisting the priest, though not on the altar, only in the vestry.[235]

The ordination to the diaconate of the Reverend Ani-Kristi Manvelian and Mayis Mateosian by Archbishop Sebouh Sarkissian, Tehran, 24 September 2017.

The Reverend Deaconess Ani-Kristi Manvelian censing during the Divine Liturgy.

---

235 This information is in the possession of the author.

Naturally, this and similar incidents, which may escalate to the point of ani-
mosity towards the ordination of women, do not contribute to the increase of
clerical ranks within the female community of believers in the Armenian
Church. After the abovementioned ordination that took place in Tehran,
Ējmiatsin's unfavourable reaction was prompt, even though the Diocese of
Iran is under the jurisdiction of the Catholicosate of the Great House of Cilicia. The response of the speaker of the Mother See, which has been published
on the pages of the Armenian press and in social media outlets, does not guar-
antee that reforms in the Armenian Church will take place to align the ecclesiastical life and its development with the spirit of today.

I mentioned above that in the early Christian communities, women
played a significant role in the mission of making Christianity a universal religion. Among them were women disciples, prophetesses, widows, and deaconesses endowed with the sevenfold gifts of the Holy Spirit. They were inspired by Christ's faith, and their activities proved immensely beneficial for
the church. However, after the proclamation of Christianity as the state religion in the Roman Empire and the church's adoption of the structure of a
state institution, women were gradually pushed away from these roles during
the Middle Ages. The church soon established a hierarchical structure based
on men, wherein women had no place at all. Naturally, this development was
also reflected in various theological commentaries, mentioning that Christ
chose his apostles only from men, that sin was brought into this world by the
woman after the creation, that Adam was created first and the woman after
him, that the woman was created from Adam's rib and thus cannot represent
God's complete image on earth. Meanwhile, in the entire universe Adam is
considered the only crown and halo of the creation and is his Creator's perfect
and true image and semblance. Women's menstruation is considered the result of sin and impurity, which is why she is seen as impure, and she is forbidden from receiving any clerical rank and ascending to the Holy Altar.

All these arguments have long lost their validity. The fact that Christ
chose his Apostles only from men and that the tradition of the church devel-
oped in this way no longer convinces many that women should be excluded
from holding clerical ranks. Christ's choice of his Apostles from only among
men was determined by the socio-cultural habits that prevailed in Israel at the
time, and when discussing this issue, this situation should be taken into con-
sideration. The tradition was shaped by the phenomena, activities, rituals, and
worship habits stemming from the demands of ecclesiastical life, which
evolved in various forms over time. Who can claim that certain phenomena

that have emerged from the demands of contemporary life, modern percep-tions, and socio-cultural relationships will not be considered a tradition in the Church after a certain period of time has passed? In Anglican, Old Catholic, Protestant, and other communities, it was only in the 19th and 20th centuries that women began to be ordained, not only as deaconesses, but also as priests and bishops. In the daily life of these churches, many deem it to be a natural phenomenon and perceive it as a tradition without which the church would lose great advantages.

The church is the home of the free and their house of prayer, where both women and men are entitled to live together under the principles of freedom and equal rights. The church should never be a domineering institution with self-justifying labels; neither spiritual nor secular. Moreover, this freedom should be reflected in the formation and unity of the church's communal life. The life of Church institutions and their daily routine should not be un-changeable and fail to improve. They should also not have repressive author-ity. That is, the right and power to suppress and constrain an individual. The Christian Church has become the realm of freedom through the Gospel while, at the same time, being guided by divine principles. It is the overall moral guardian of human freedom in the world. So that the church, with its male-dominated structures, can become everybody's church, all the decision-mak-ing spiritual and administrative bodies should yet again widely embrace the inclusion of women. Women should hold a substantial role and actively par-ticipate in the spiritual and administrative life of the church.

There are no compelling arguments or fundamental theological contra-dictions to oppose the demand for women to hold spiritual offices. Given the leading roles that women played in the first centuries of the church's exist-ence, as well as their rightfully improved positions in the economy, science, culture, politics, statehood, and society, it is simply illogical and detrimental for the church to adopt a non-compromising, unfavourable, and even hostile attitude towards women.

The history of the newly founded church in the earliest centuries demon-strates that the recently converted Christians deliberately avoided using secu-lar titles when assuming various offices or responsibilities in the Church, be-cause all those honorifics inherently contained elements of domination, sub-jugation, and command. Instead, the church found a practical solution that was derived from the divine principles bequeathed by Christ. As such, the church adopted the term ministry to refer to the Christian calling. The Gos-pel's Greek original has preserved it in its humblest but most resonant form: διακονία = διάκονος = διακόνισσα, which our Classical Armenian translates as *sarkawagut'iwn, sarkawag,* and *sarkawaguhi,* meaning "to serve or assist one's companions.": "The greatest among you will be your servant" (Mt 23:11)[236]. This was Christ's counsel to his Apostles and followers. It was, therefore, not at all accidental that the church's first "officials", who were chosen in the presence of the Apostles and Christ's disciples, were seven deacons whose main responsibility was to serve. Ministry is the best characteristic of the office that the church bestows. But it does not denote an honorific, princely, or noble title, but rather an activity. That activity is the love of Christian service. Indeed, the primary authority of the Church lies in its commitment to service.[237]

As previously noted, in early Christian church communities, the diaconate was practised by both men and women, for example, deaconesses Phoebe and Prisca mentioned in Apostle Paul's epistles (Rom 16:1, 3). Before the fall of the Eastern Roman Empire, there were women deacons who, in addition to serving at the Holy Altar during the liturgy and assisting during the baptism of girls, also performed the duties equivalent to the service responsibilities of male deacons.

Concerning Christian open-mindedness and equality between the sexes, in contrast to other influential churches that were established by the Apostles, the Armenian Church managed to preserve the tradition of women's diaconate within its ranks, providing women with an opportunity to serve at the Holy Altar and to commit themselves to various Christian services within the life of the church. It would be sorrowful if, in the near future, this tradition that brings joyful dew to our spiritual landscape ceased to exist in the Armenian Church. Yet the respectable Ani-Kristi Manvelian mentioned earlier is the last female "Mohican" and the only deaconess of the contemporary Armenian Apostolic Church. The future is uncertain, and, in this respect, the parched field of our church needs rejuvenating rain. This largely depends on the positive orientation of our church's clerical elite. But more so, it will be determined by the major demand from the larger circles of our devout people and by the readiness to receive titles born in our church's spirit-revitalising font. This will ensure that deaconesses will become a valuable and significant presence in the church's clerical ranks through ordination.

Within this context, a question arises: why is there currently a shortage of the necessary components to maintain a continuous and sufficient number

---

236 Cf. also Mk 9:34.
237 See Küng, Hans, *Die Frau im Christentum*, ibid., p. 20.

of deaconesses in the service of our church? Numerous reasons may be provided, but I will limit myself to only a few aspects of our church that need to be revised or considered more fully:

i. The power of the Church should not be centralised only in the hands of men, especially the celibate ones.

ii. In certain circles in our society and of power-hungry clergy, outdated stereotypes exist of women being feeble and unclean due to menstruation. This mentality should change.

iii. Treating women as if they exist solely to satisfy sexual needs or function merely as childbearing creatures must be stopped. It is fallacious to associate someone's sexuality with the original or inherited sin. Sexuality is an integral part of someone's life and identity, which God bestowed equally upon man and woman. Man and woman, not only with their intellectual and spiritual advantages but also in the flesh, are created with a mission to complete each other, make each other whole, and become one flesh in love – "and the two will become one flesh" (Gn 2:24; Mt 19:5; Mk 10:8; Eph 5:31). Before God, man and woman are of equal value. They were both created in the image of God, and on earth, they jointly represent the image of their creator, God. Both are endowed with the same intellectual, ethical, and spiritual abilities and have the same responsibilities and missions on earth.

iv. The office of diaconate is not equally open to both men and women with a spiritual calling, but it should be. The condition for ordaining someone as a deacon should be based on the individual's spiritual vocation and educational preparation rather than on sexual differences.

v. The service of deaconesses should not be limited exclusively to nunneries and female abbacies. The service mission of both deaconesses and their male counterparts should be treated as equal. They should enjoy the same rights, such as serving at the altar, offering spiritual education, teaching, taking care of orphans, and providing different services to the sick, the grieving, the needy, and the older people. In other words, the presence of deaconesses in the church's social life should be substantial and even indispensable.

vi. From the upper echelons of the church to dioceses and pastorates, everyone should encourage and promote women's spiritual and ecclesiastical service, bestowing the four clerical ranks, the offices of subdiaconate and then diaconate on female candidates with a vocation or suitable training.

vii. For this programme to succeed and bud in the fields of the church and then bear fruit, the diaconate should certainly reflect the spirit of the time. This means that celibacy should not be a mandatory requirement to ordain women as deaconesses. As is the case with male deacons, individuals should be free to make their decisions and, based on their preference and vocation, choose whether they want to be celibate or married when carrying out their pastoral service.

viii. Discrimination based on sex is foreign to the spirit of the church and hinders its redemptive mission. It is reactionary in essence and prevents the church from developing according to the spirit of the time. The exceptionally male elite of our church should recognise the spirit of the time and positively approach the handling of all challenges. The church exists through a large multitude of its believers and their active engagement, not just through the orders of its male elite.

A faithful Armenian woman should not be limited only to the "women's guild" of the diocese or parish; organising fairs, running stalls, cooking, preparing savoury dishes, and doing needlework to ensure the church's income. They should also be included in the church's ritualistic and missionary practices with the spiritual calling and superior rank bestowed on them, one of which at least could be that of a deaconess.

ix. Both deacon and deaconess, having the same missionary and ritualistic rights, are called to serve the Church of Christ. It goes against Christian beliefs to turn this office, which is unequivocally all about servicing, into a position of authority, to attribute certain powers to it, and to exploit it for either appropriate or inappropriate reasons. This must not be legitimised in the church. As the Apostle says, faith is realised through works.[238] Therefore, it is a great sin to deprive a woman of expressing her heart's living faith through the preaching of the Word of life, worship, and testimony of faith solely based on differences in sex. On this topic, one of our eminent fathers, *vardapet* Barsegh Mashkeworts'i, said in his commentary of the Gospel of Mark: "Because not only is it our duty to admonish and educate, but also *you all, men and women accomplished in age*, should teach the imperfect and the simple-minded with words and works. And if you fail to do so, both you and we are in the same sin. Therefore, admonish them with the virtuous works of illumination..."[239]

---

238 Cf. Jas 2:14-20: "What good is it, my brothers and sisters, if you say you have faith but do not have works? Can faith save you? [...] faith by itself, if it has no works, is dead. [...] Do you want to be shown, you senseless person, that faith apart from works is barren?".

239 Barsegh *vardapet* (Mashkeworts'i), *Meknut'iwn Srboy Awetaranin or ĕst Markosi*, p. 457: Զի ո՛չ թէ մեզ միայն եմք պարտական խրատել եւ ուսուցանել, այլ եւ ամենայնքն՝ արթ եւ կանայք՝ կատարեալքդ հասակաւ պարտիք ուսուցանել զանկատարսն եւ զտղայաբարոյսն՝ բանիւք եւ գործովք. զոր թէ ո՛չ առնէք՝

x. Of course, it is evident to any reasonable person that the question of women being part of the church's hierarchy starts with the diaconate but does not end there. Currently, the question pertains to the revival of the sacred tradition of deaconess, which is dying but has existed in the history of our Church for centuries. But the demand for women to attain the title and authority of a priest and a bishop will logically follow the diaconate. Are the representatives of our ecclesiastical elite ready to share the church's spiritual and administrative authority with women on equal terms? If this question is not necessarily answered today or tomorrow, it must be answered in the future. If it remains unanswered, it does not stop being a serious and contemporary issue.

In conclusion, we must not only echo, but also deeply contemplate the words bequeathed to us by our enlightened forebears. These are words that came from individuals of visionary prowess and remarkably open minds, who transcended the limitations imposed by societal and cultural norms: "Do not regard this as something new and irregular, because we have learned it from the tradition of the holy apostle, since he says: "I entrust to you Phoebe our sister, who is a servant of the church" (Mkhit'ar Gosh).

ընդ նովին մեղադրութեամբ էք եւ դուք որպէս եւ մեք: Արդ՝ խրատեցուք զնոսա լուաւոր գործովքն առաքինութեան ...:

Photographic Documentation

St Katarinē's Convent of New Julfa

Five nuns of St Katarinē's Convent of New Julfa. To the right, stands a novice with a habit and a cowl-like cover on her head, 19th century.

Blessing of Grapes in New Julfa with the participation of deaconesses from St Katarinē's Convent. Photo by Ernst Hoeltzer, 1881.

Nuns clacking the wooden clappers, inviting people to the church.

Deaconess Eghisabēt' Israyēlean, sister of Patriarch Kiwregh Israyēlean, most probably one the last abbess of St Katarinē's Convent of New Julfa (Sion, 10-12, 1945, p. 165).

A nun from St Katarinē's Convent, with a stole on her right shoulder, holding a candle.

Deaconesses and nuns with a celebrant priest.

Document regarding St Katarinē's Convent of New Julfa, which was passed on by Arshak Alpoyachean to the abbess Aghawni K'eoseyan on the occasion of his visit to Cairo (Hay Khōsnak, 5-6, 1933, pp. 80-81).

St Step'anos's Convent of Tbilisi

St Step'anos Church, also known by the name Khojivank' and by its historical exterior.

St Step'anos Church in 1980, after it was converted to Georgian. Now it is called Kvemo Bethlehem Saviour's Nativity Church (ქვემო ბეთლეჰმი). This photographic evidence serves as a poignant testament to cultural genocide. All inscriptions in Armenian have been removed from the walls and the bas-reliefs have been destroyed to transform the church completely (see Karapetyan, Samvel, Vrats' petakan k'aghak'akanut'yunĕ ew hay mshakuyt'i husharjannerĕ (1988-1998) (The state policy of Georgia and the monuments of Armenian Culture (1988-1998), Yerevan, 1998, p. 37).

Abbess, princess, archdeaconess Hṛipʻsimē Aghekʻ-Tʻahireantsʻ (1847-1934).

Nuns of St Stepʻanos Convent of Tbilisi, Tbilisi, 1914.

The former entrance of St Step'anos Convent.

The cupola of St Step'anos Convent.

The cupola of St Step'anos Convent featuring a carved busts of nuns.

Inscription: *"This stone of the holy cathedral of the nunnery is a memorial of the Eavanguleants' family in 1870."*

Inscription: *"This washing font was constructed through the personal assets of Reverend dpruhi Anna Khojaminasean in memory of her parents in the year 1870."*

Inscription: "*By the grace of Almighty God, I, virgin P'ep'ronia, daughter of Agha Karapet Khubeants' from Yerevan, had the dome of this cathedral covered on August 15, 1885, during the patriarchate of Lord Makar T'[eghutts'i] through my personal assets in memory of both my late parents and myself. And I entered the hermitage in the glory of God in the year 1826, during the abbacy of Yustianē, and I was professed in the year 1846, during the leadership of Archbishop Karapet and the patriarchate of Lord Nersēs V and the abbacy of Gayianē Behbut'eants', since the year 1871 up to the present day I have held the position of senior sacristan in the cathedral of the Lord.*"

Inscription: "By the grace of the Almighty Lord God, I, deaconess Hṛipʻsimē Bēgtʻabegeantsʻ, a colleague of the Abbess of the nunnery of Tbilisi, erected this stone column of the holy cathedral through my own assets in memory of my parents, myself, and nun Nunē Babanaseantsʻ, whom the Lord received for His pleasure. Amen. Year 1870."

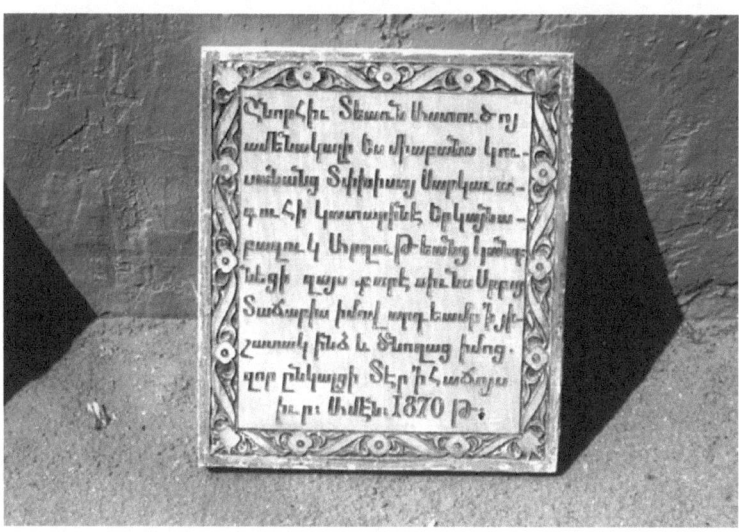

Inscription: "By the grace of the Almighty Lord God, I, a nun of the Tbilisi nunnery, Deaconess Katarinē Erkaynabazuk Arghut'eants', erected this stone column of the holy cathedral through my own assets in memory of both my parents and myself; may this please the Lord. Amen. Year 1870."

Inscription: "The stairs of the cathedral door were built through the assets and expenses of the late Abbess of the Armenian nunnery of Tbilisi, Archdeaconess virgin Ewp'imeay of the princely Bēhbut'eants' [family], in the year 1885, 17 August."

Inscription: "The stairs of the cathedral door were built through the assets and expenses of the late Abbess of the Armenian nunnery of Tbilisi, Archdeaconess virgin Ewpʻimeay of the princely Bēhbutʻeantsʻ [family], in the year 1885, 17 August."

Inscription: *"By the grace of the Almighty God, I, Deaconess Gayianē Bēhbut'eants', Abbess of St Step'anos Convent of Tbilisi, bequeathed 8,000 to St Step'anos Church of this institution for my wealth (?) from my late brother, general-lieutenant Dawit' Yovsep'ean Bēhbudeants' in memory of him and myself, looking forward to being rewarded by the Lord at a later time. In the year 1868."*

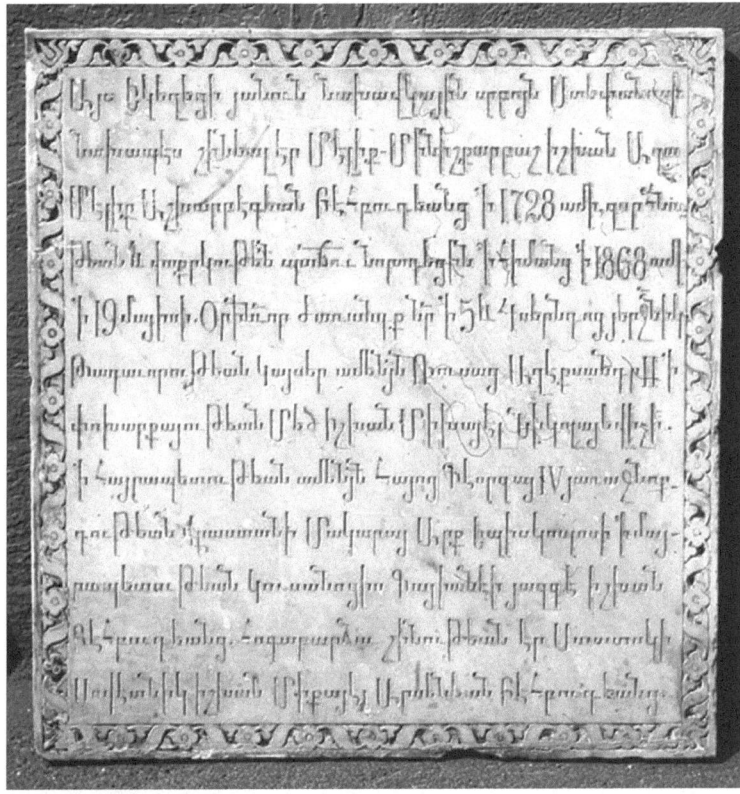

Inscription: *"This church, dedicated to the Protomartyr St Step'anos, was initially constructed by Prince Mēlik'-Minishk'abash Agha Mēlik' Ashkharbēgean Bēhbudeants' in the year 1728; it was rebuilt from its foundations on May 19, 1868, due to its age and small size. His legal heirs of the fifth and fourth generation, during the blessed reign of the Emperor of All Russia Alexander II, the viceroyalty of Grand Duke Michael Nikolaevich, during the patriarchate of [the Catholicos of] All Armenians Gēorg IV, under the prelacy of Archbishop Makar of Georgia, during the abbacy of Gayianē from the family of prince Bēhbudeants' in the nunnery; the overseer of the construction was the State Counsellor prince Mik'ayēl Arsenean Bēhbudeants'."*

Inscription: "*This church of the Protomartyr St Step'anos of Tbilisi's Armenian nunnery, built in 1728, renovated in 1868, was again renovated from both inside and outside in accordance with the ancient Armenian church style, by the decision of His Holiness Catholicos Matt'ēos II Izmirlean, through the financial support of the Abbess of this hermitage Yep'rosinē of the princely family of Abamēlik'ean. This renovation took place in the days of the Governor-General of the Caucasus Viceroyalty Count I. I. Varants'ov-Dashkov and the prelacy of Archbishop Garegin Sat'unean.*"

Another disturbing piece of evidence of cultural genocide, in that it provides the memory of the poignant melody of the Antuni song.

The Orphan-Nurturing Sisters of the Galfayean Community

Srbuhi Nshan-Galfayean, founder of the Galfayean community of orphan-nurturers (1822-1889).

The Galfayean sisters with the trustees and His Beatitude Archbishop Shnorhk'
Galustean. The photo was taken on the occasion of the 100th anniversary of the community's foundation in 1966.

The Galfayean sisters and deaconesses with His Beatitude Archbishop Shnorhk'
Galustean. All are wearing the liturgy vestments.

Ordination of subdeaconesses by His Beatitude Archbishop Shnorhkʻ Galustean. The Holy Trinity Church, Constantinople, 1966.

Ordination of Archdeaconess Mother Mariam Kʻēōsēean.

The Galfayean sisters with Archdeaconess Mother Mariam Kʻēōsēean.

Archdeaconess Mother Mariam Kʻēōsēean censing the holy altar.

Sister Zarmuhi Mehrapean singing the liturgy with the Galfayean pupils.

Sister Nēvrik Pasmanean, January 8, 1925.

The Galfayean deaconesses presenting the Holy Chalice for communion during the Divine Liturgy.

The orphan-nurturing Galfayean sisters with their Mother Superior Mariam K'ēōsēean in 1964.

Sitting: Mother Aghawni K'ēōsēean. At the back, from left to right: Zarmuhi Mehrapean, Nēvrik Pasmanean, Mariam K'ēōsēean, and Aruseak Mkhit'arean.

Archdeaconess Sister Hṛip'simē Sasunean in 1954.

The deaconesses and subdeaconesses of the Galfayean Community of orphan-nurturers.

The deaconesses and subdeaconesses of the Galfayean Community of Orphan-Nurturers wearing festive robes and stoles. This photo was taken in front of the former St Step'anos Church of Khasgiwgh. The church was a glorious temple, nationalised by the Turkish government during the construction of the second bridge of Oskejiwr. The four nuns, from left to right, are: Sister Zarmuhi Mehrapean, Mother Mariam K'ēosēean, Sister Nēvrik Pasmanean, Mother Aghawni K'ēosēean. (For clarifications regarding this photo, I would like to express my special gratitude to Reverend Grigor Tamatean).

*Archdeaconess Sister Hṛipʿsimē Sasunean presenting the Holy Chalice for commun-
ion to the celebrant Archbishop Mesrop Mutʿafean. Musa Dagh, village of Vakʿēf
(Vakıflı), Church of the Holy Mother of God, 1985.*

Bibliography

List of Manuscripts

MS Galata, Armenian National Library 237

MS Matenadaran 39

MS Matenadaran 907

MS Matenadaran 953

MS Matenadaran 954

MS Matenadaran 960

MS Matenadaran 962

MS Matenadaran 970

MS Matenadaran 998

MS Matenadaran 1455

MS Matenadaran 1712

MS Matenadaran 1735

MS Matenadaran 2404

MS Matenadaran 2787

MS Matenadaran 3508

MS Matenadaran 4088

MS Matenadaran 4195

MS Matenadaran 4363

MS Matenadaran 4961

MS Matenadaran 5153

MS Matenadaran 6450

MS Matenadaran 8075

MS Matenadaran 9240

MS Venice 199

MS Venice 457

MS Vienna 931

Literature

Abēl Abeghay (a.k.a. Manoukian), *Hay ekeghetsʻu sarkawaguhinerĕ* (The Deacon-esses of the Armenian Church), New York, 1991.

Achelis, Hans and Johannes Flemming (trans. and eds.), *Die Syrische Didaskalia*, Leipzig, 1904.

Aghawnuni, Mkrtichʻ, *Miabankʻ ew aytsʻelukʻ hay Erusaghēmi* (Monks and Visi-tors of Armenian Jerusalem), Jerusalem, 1929.

Akinean, Nersēs, *Movsēs III Tatʻewatsʻi Hayotsʻ Katʻoghikosn ew ir zhamanakĕ: Npast mĕ Hayotsʻ ekeghetsʻwoy patmutʻean 1577-1633 shrjani hamar* (Cathol-icos Movsēs III Tatʻewatsʻi and His Time: A Contribution to Armenian Ec-clesiastical History for the Period 1577-1633), Vienna, 1936.

Alishan, Ghewond, *Sisakan: Teghagrutʻiwn Siwneatsʻashkharhi* (Sisakan: The To-pography of the Land of Siwnikʻ), Venice, 1893.

Alpōyachean, Arshak, *Hay Khōsnak* (Armenian Speaker), IX, 5-6, 1933, pp. 80-81.

Anonymous, *Vatʻsunameak (1866-1926) Galfayean aghjkantsʻ orbanotsʻi* (60th Anniversary (1866-1926) of the Galfayean Girls' Orphanage), Khasgiwgh.

Anonymous, *Galfayean aghjkantsʻ orbanotsʻ (1866-1934)* (Galfayean Girls' Or-phanage [1866-1934]), Constantinople, 1935.

Aṛakʻel Davrizhetsʻi, *Patmutʻiwn Aṛakʻel Vardapeti Dawrizhetsʻwoy* (History of the Vardapet Arakʻel Davrizhetsʻi), Vagharshapat, 1896.

Araratyan Hayrapetakan Tʻem, Zoravor Surb Astvatsatsin Ekeghetsʻi, "Gavazan" (Crosier), published online on 29 April 2015, <https://surbzoravor.am/post/view/gavazan≥, accessed on 18 January 2024.

Arat, Mari Kristin, „Die Diakonissen der armenischen Kirche aus kanonischer Sicht", *Handēs Amsōreay*, 1-12, 1987, pp. 153-190.

Arevshatyan, Anna, "Khosrovidukht", *Kʻristonya Hayastan Hanragitaran*, Yere-van, 2002.

—, "Stepʻanos Siwnetsʻu varkʻĕ orpes vaghkʻristoneakan Hayastani erazhshtakan arvesti arzhekʻavor patmakan aghbyur" (The Vita of Stepʻanos Siwnetsʻi as a Valuable Source of Early Christian Armenia's Musical Art), *Banber Matena-darani* 30, 2020.

Arzumanyan, M.V. et al (eds.), *Haykakan Sovetakan Hanragitaran* (Soviet Arme-nian Encyclopaedia), Vol. VIII, Yerevan, 1982.

Awetikʻean, Gabriel, Siwrmelean, Khachʻatur, and Mkrtichʻ Awgerean (eds.), *Nor Baṛgirkʻ Haykazean Lezui* (New Dictionary of the Armenian Language), Vol. II, Yerevan, 1981.

Aw. H., "Hay keankʻ ew ekeghetsʻi: Norin Vehapʻaṛutʻiwn T. T. Gēorg V Amenayn Hayotsʻ Katʻoghikosi anuanakochʻutʻiwnĕ, Gēorgean H. chemarani tōnĕ ew s. Miwṛōni ōrhnutiwnĕ" (Armenian Life and Church: The Adoption of the

Name of His Holiness Supreme Patriarch and Catholicos of All Armenians Gēorg V, the Feast of the Gevork'yan Theological Seminary, and the Blessing of the Holy Myrrh), *Ararat* 10-11, 1912, pp. 879-891.

Ayvazean, Abraham, *Shar Hay Kensagrut'eants'* (A Series of Armenian Biographies), Constantinople, 1893.

—, "Awag sarkawaguhi mě i Sēōlēōz" (An Archdeaconess from Sēōlēōz), *Hay Khōsnak*, 5-6, 1933.

Aznaworean, Zareh, *Hay Ekeghets'in 20-rd darun ew 21-rd daru shemin* (Armenian Church in the 20th Century and at the Threshold of the 21st Century), Nicosia, 2005.

Barącz, Sadok, *Żywoty sławnych Ormian w Polsce* (Lives of famous Armenians in Poland), Lwów, 1856.

Barkhutareants', Makar, *Artsakh*, Bagu, 1895.

Barsegh *vardapet* (Mashkeworts'i), *Meknut'iwn Srboy Awetaranin or ěst Markosi* (Commentary on the Holy Gospel by Mark), Vol. II, Constantinople, 1826.

Barseghyan, Bella, "Lehahayots' kronakan hamaynk'" (The Armenian Religious Community of Poland), *K'ristonya Hayastan*, Yerevan, 2002.

Bēylik'chean, Melik', "Awag arkawaguhiner hay kusastanneri mej" (Archdeaconesses in Armenian Nunneries), *Hayrenik' Ōragir*, 26 November 1895.

—, "Awag arkawaguhiner hay kusastanneri mej" (Archdeaconesses in Armenian Nunneries), *Hay Khōsnak*, IX, 5-6, 1933, pp. 79-82.

Blank, Joseph, *Frauen in den Jesusüberlieferungen*, in: *Die Frau im Urchristentum*, hrsg. v. Gerhard Dautzenberg, Helmut Merklein, Karlheinz Müller, Freiburg, Basel, Wien, 1989.

Ch'ēpēyean, Ghewond, "Sarkavaguhinerě Hayots' Ekeghets'u mēj" (Deaconesses in the Armenian Church), *Hask* 4-5, 1989, pp. 169-171.

Connolly, Hugh R. (trans.), *Didascalia Apostolorum: The Syriac Version Translated and Accompanied by the Verona Latin Fragments*, Oxford, 1929.

Cooper, James and Arthur J. Maclean (trans. and eds.), *The Testament of Our Lord*, Edinburgh, 1902.

Corley, Felix, "Zernov and the Armenian Deaconesses of Tiflis", 2022, <https://www.academia.edu/83293238/>, accessed on 18 January 2024.

Cuhaj, George S. (ed.), *Standard Catalog of World Coins: 1801-1900*, 6th ed., Iola, Wi., 2009.

Editors, "Koys H. T'ayireani Nuěrě" (The Gift of Nun H. T'ayirean), *Lumay* 3, 1903, p. 271.

Editors, "Mayr At'oṛ" (Mother See), *Ararat* 10-11, 1912, p. 1051.

Editors, "Mayr At'oṛum" (In the Mother See), *Ējmiatsin* 10, 1953, pp. 15-16.

Editors, "Kat'oghikos" (Catholicos), *K'ristonya Hayastan*, Yerevan, 2002, pp. 457-470.

Ervine, R. Roberta, "The Armenian Church's Women Deacons", *St. Nersess Theological Review* 12, 2007, pp. 17-56.

Ezeants', Karapet (trans. and ed.), *Brni miut'iwn Hayots' Lehastani ĕnd Ekeghets'woyn Hromay. Zhamanakakits' yishatakarank'* (Forced Union of the Armenians of Poland with the Roman Church: Contemporary Memoires), St Petersburg, 1884.

Eznik Koghbats'i, *Eghts Aghandots'* (Against the Sects), Yerevan, 1994.

Galachean, S., "Hay Ekeghets'woy sarkawaguhinerĕ erēk ew aysōr" (The Deaconesses of the Armenian Church, Yesterday and Today), *Zhamanak Daily*, December 23, 2017.

Galstyan, A.G., *Datastanagirk'* (Book of Judgement), Yerevan, 1958.

Grigor Tat'ewats'i, *Girk' Harts'mants'* (Book of Questions), Constantinople, 1729.

Gröne, Valentin (trans.), *Tatian's, des Kirchenschriftstellers, Rede an die Griechen*, Bibliothek der Kirchenväter, 1 Serie, Band 28, Kempten, 1872.

Hakobyan, G.A., "8-rd dari mer kin sharakanagirnerĕ" (Our Eighth-Century Women Authors of *Sharakans*), *Ējmiatsin* 34(3), 1977.

Hakobyan, Vazgen (ed.), *Hayeren dzeragreri ZhĒ dari hishatakaranner (1641-1660)* (The Colophons of Armenian Manuscripts of the 17th Century [1641-1660]), Vol. III, Yerevan, 1984.

— (ed.), *Kanonagirk' Hayots'* (The Book of Canon Law of Armenians), Vol. I, Yerevan, 1964.

— (ed.), *Kanonagirk' Hayots'* (The Book of Canon Law of Armenians), Vol. II, Yerevan, 1971.

Harut'yunyan, Arsen, *Vagharshapat: Vank'erĕ ew vimagrut'yunnerĕ* (Vagharshapat: The Monasteries and the Epigraphic Data), Holy Ējmiatsin, 2016.

Hats'uni, Vardan, *Hayuhin Patmut'ean Arjew* (The Armenian Woman Facing History), Venice, 1936.

—, *Patmut'iwn hin hay tarazin* (History of the Ancient Armenian Dress), Venice, 1923.

Höfer, Josef and Rahner, Karl (eds.), *Lexikon für Theologie und Kirche*, Vol. III, Freiburg, 1959.

Hovhannisyan, Petros, "Lehastani haykakan gaght'avayrerĕ XVI-XVII darerum (gaght'akanut'yan ughinerĕ, zhamanakĕ, teghabashkhumĕ, t'vak'anakĕ, zbaghmuk'ĕ)" (The Armenian Settlements in Poland in 16th–17th Centuries [Routes of Emigration, Time, Distribution, Number, Occupation]), *Ējmiatsin* 1, 2009.

Israyēlean, Kiwregh, "Nor-Jughayi S. Katarinēan Anapatĕ" (The St Katarinē Hermitage of New Julfa), *Sion*, 10-12, 1944, pp. 192-199.

—, "Nor-Jughayi S. Katarinēan Anapatĕ" (The St Katarinē Hermitage of New Julfa), *Sion*, 1, 1945, pp. 23-27.

Jalaleants', Sargis, *Chanaparhordut'iwn i Metsn Hayastan* (A Journey to Greater Armenia), Vol. II, Tbilisi, 1858.

Katholische Kirche, Bistum Limburg, "Ring und Stab für die Hirtin der Abtei: Sr. Katharina Drouvé hat von Bischof Bätzing die Äbtissinnenweihe empfangen", published online on 5 March 2023, <https://bistumlimburg.de/beitrag/ring-und-stab-fuer-die-hirtin-der-abtei-1/>, accessed on 18 January 2024.

Kellner, Heinrich (trans.), *Tertullian, private und katechetische Schriften*, Bibliothek der Kirchenväter, 1. Reihe, Band 7, München 1912.

Kʻēōpʻriwlean Vuicic, Pronislawa, "Lehastani hay patmakan yishstakaranneru tsʻutsʻahandēsě" (The Exhibition of Armenian Historical Artifacts of Poland), *Anahit* 3-6, 1932-1933, pp. 38-53.

Kʻēōsēean, Y., "Sahakdukht Siwnetsʻi", *Matenagirkʻ Hayotsʻ*, VI, 8ᵗʰ Century, Antelias, Lebanon, 2007.

Khachʻatryan, Vardan, "Haykakan gaghtʻavayrerě mijnadarum. Lehastan ew Arewmtyan Ukraina" (The Armenian Diaspora in Middle Ages: Poland and Western Ukraine), *Hayotsʻ Patmutʻiwn* (History of Armenia), Vol. II, Book II (second half of the 9ᵗʰ c.–first half of the 17ᵗʰ c.), Yerevan, 2014.

Kharatean, Henrik, "Tʻiblisi S. Stepʻanos kusanatsʻ anapati ew mayrapet ishkhanuhi Hripʻsimē Tʻahireantsʻi masin (About St Stepʻanos nunnery and Hripʻsimē Tʻahireantsʻ, the Abbess Princess)", *Ējmiatsin* 5, 2007, pp. 87-91.

Khutsʻean, Khorēn, *Tʻiflisi S. Stepʻanos kusanatsʻ anapati patmutʻiwně* (The History of the St Stepʻanos Nunnery of Tiflis), Tbilisi, 1914.

Kirakos Gandzaketsʻi, *Kirakos vardapeti Gandzaketsʻwoy hamaṛōt patmutʻiwn i srboy Grigorē yawurs iwr lusabaneal* (A Brief History from St Grigor until His Days Explained), Venice, 1865.

Kiwlesērean, Babgēn, *Patmutʻiwn Katʻoghikosatsʻ Kilikioy. 1441-ēn minchew mer ōrerě* (History of the Catholicoi of Cilicia: From 1441 up to the Present Day), Antelias, 1939.

Küng, Hans, *Die Frau im Christentum*, Zürich, 2001.

L'Huillier, Peter, *The Church of the Ancient Councils: The Disciplinary Work of the First Four Ecumenical Councils*. Crestwood, NY, 1996.

Lynch, Henry F.B., *Armenia: Travels and Studies*, Vol. I, London, 1901.

Malkhaseantsʻ, Stepʻan (ed.), *Hayerēn Batsʻatrakan Baṛaran* (Dictionary of Armenian Language), Vol. IV, Yerevan, 1944.

Margarean, Grigor, *Kensagrutʻiwn Srbuhi Mayrapeti Nshan-Galfayean. Himnadir-mayr hamanun orbanotsʻi aghjkantsʻ hastateal i Khasgiwgh 1 Yunuar 1866* (Biography of the Abbess Srbuhi Nshan-Galfayean: Mother-Founder of the Homonymous Girls' Orphanage established in Khasgiwgh on 1 January 1866), Constantinople, 1892.

Mayer, Josephine (ed.), *Monumenta de viduis diaconissis virginibusque tractantia. Collegit notis et prolegomenis instruxit* (= Florilegium Patristicum), Bd. 42, Bonn, 1938.

Mayr, Michael (trans.), "Die Weihe von Frauen zu Diakoninnen", *Wijngaards Institute for Catholic Research*, <https://womenpriests.org/de/tradition-de/ deac-ord-die-weihe-von-frauen-%20zu-diakoninnen/>, accessed on 15 January 2024.

Melikʻ-Tʻangean, Nersēs, *Hayotsʻ ekeghetsʻakan irawunkʻĕ* (The Canon Law of the Armenian Church), Vol. I, Shushi, 1903

—, *Hayotsʻ ekeghetsʻakan irawunkʻĕ* (The Canon Law of the Armenian Church), Vol. II, Shushi, 1905.

Meneshian, O. Knarik, "A Nearly Forgotten History: Women Deacons in the Armenian Church", *The Armenian weekly*", 6 July 2013, <https://armenian weekly.com/2013/07/06/a-nearly-forgotten-history-women-deacons-in-the -armenian-church/>, accessed on 16 January 2024.

Mikʻaelyan, Davitʻ, "Averum en moṛatsʻutʻyunitsʻ pʻrkvats verjin nshkharnerĕ: Inchʻ en hushum Shushii haykakan gerezmanotsʻi vimagir ardzanagrutʻyunnerĕ" (They are destroying the last remnants saved from oblivion: What do the inscriptions from the Armenian cemetery of Shushi relate?), *Hayastani Hanrapetutʻyun*, 11 September, 2021, <https://hhpress. am/taratsashrjan/2021 /5532/>, accessed on 16 January 2024.

Minasyan, Tamara, "Artsakhi dzeṛagrakan zhaṛangutʻyunĕ" (The Manuscript Tradition of Artsakh), in *Das armenische Kulturerbe in Berg-Karabach/ Arzach und die* Deutschen, Martin Tamcke et al (eds.), Göttingen, 2021, pp. 47-60.

Mkhitʻar Gosh, *Datastanagirkʻ of Mxitʻar Goš*, translated by Robert W. Thomson, Amsterdam, 2000, p. 278.

—, *Girkʻ Datastani* (Book of Judgement), edited by Khosrov Tʻorosyan, Yerevan, 1975.

Mkhitʻareantsʻ, Abēl, *Patmutʻiwn Zhoghovotsʻ Hayastaneaytsʻ Ekeghetsʻwoy* (History of the Councils of the Armenian Church), Vagharshapat, 1874.

Mkrtchʻyan, Heghine, "Kusanatsʻ lkʻvats anapatneri sarkavaguhinerĕ" (The Deaconesses of Abandoned Female Hermitages), Published 24 February, 2016, <https://ter-hambardzum.net/կուսանաց-լքված-անապատներիսարկավագն/>, accessed on 16 January 2024.

—, "Sarkavaguhineri tsaṛayutʻyunn u pashtonĕ Hay aṛakʻelakan ekeghetsʻum" (The Service and the Office of Deaconesses in the Armenian Apostolic Church), *Ējmiatsin* 10, 2013, pp. 39-51.

Movsēs Erznkatsʻi, "Ĕnddimadrutʻiwn saks jroyn kharṇman i surb khorhurdn. i tʻuis hayotsʻ 558 (= 1309 CE)" (Refutation of Mixing Water in the Holy Eucharist of the year 1309), MS Matenadaran 8075.

Navoyan, Mher, "Sahakdukht", *Kʻristonya Hayastan Hanragitaran*, Yerevan, 2002.

Nersēs Lambronats'i, *Khorhrdatsut'iwnk' i kargs ekeghets'woy ew meknut'iwn khorhrdoy pataragin* (Deliberations on the Church Orders and an Exegesis of the Mystery of the Liturgy), Venice, 1847.

Ōghlugean (Manukean), Abēl, *Matenagrakan hetazōtut'iwnner Movsēs vardapet Erznkats'u grakan areghtsuatsi shurj* (Literary Studies regarding the Literary Mystery of *Movsēs vardapet Erznkats'i*), Ējmiatsin, 2001.

Oghlukian (a.k.a. Manoukian) A., *The Deaconess in the Armenian Church: A Brief Survey*, trans. S. Peter Cowe, New York, 1994.

Ōrmanean, Maghak'ia, *Azgapatum* (National History), Vol. I, Constantinople, 1913.

—, *Azgapatum* (National History), Vol. II, Constantinople, 1914.

Perch Ērziean, Ch'inar Yakob, *Haryurameay yishatakaran Galfayean tan 1866-1966* (The One Hundred Year Commemoration of the House of Galfayean 1866-1966), Istanbul, 1966.

Pharr, Clyde (ed. and trans.), *The Theodosian Code and Novels and the Sirmondian Constitutions*. Princeton, 1952.

Pliny, *C. Plini Caecili Secundi, Epistularum*, edited by Elmer Truesdell Merrill, Leipzig 1922.

Pogharyan, Norayr, "Hay grch'uhiner" (Armenian Women Scribes), *Sion*, IV-V, 1954, pp. 133-134.

Pōghos Tarōnets'i, *T'ught' eranelwoyn Pōghosi Tarōnats'oy yaght'ōgh akhoyean vardapeti ĕnd dēm T'ēop'isteay Horom P'ilisop'ayin* (Epistle of the Blessed Pōghos Tarōnets'i, the Winner Adversary of the Roman Philosopher Theopistos), Constantinople, 1752.

Pogossian, Zaroui, "Women at the Beginning of Christianity in Armenia", *Orientalia Christiana Periodica* 69, 2003, pp. 355-380.

Polatean, Derenik, "Ugheworut'iwn i S. Ējmiatsin" (Journey to Holy Ējmiatsin), *Hask* 1, 1954, pp. 9-23.

Rahmani, Ephrem, *Testamentum Domini nostri Jesu Christi nunc primum editur, latine reddidit et illustravit*, Mainz, 1899.

Roberts, Alexander and James Donaldson (eds.), *The Writings of the Fathers Down to AD 325*, Ante-Nicene Fathers, Vol. VII. Book II, xxv, Peabody, MA, 1995.

Sargisean, Barsegh and Grigor Sargisean (eds.), *Mayr ts'uts'ak hayerēn dzeragrats' i Venetik* (Catalogue of Armenian Manuscripts of Venice), Vol. III, Venice, 1966.

Sayegh, Ara, "Lehahay gawazanakir miandznuhiner" (Polish-Armenian Crosier-Carrying Nuns), *Hayrenik'*, 18 May 2023, <https://hairenikweekly.com/?p=56239>, accessed on 15 January 2024.

Schäfer, Joachim, "Kassia die Hymnographin", *Ökumenische Heiligenlexikon*, <https://www.heiligenlexikon.de/BiographienK/Kassia_Hymnographin.html>, accessed on 15 January, 2024.

Shirinian, Manea-Ėrna S., "Saakdukht Siunetsi", *Pravoslavnaia Ėntsikoplediia*, Vol. LX, Moscow, 2020.

Shirinyan, Ėṛna, "Aṛajin kin sharakanagirnerĕ" (The Fist Women Authors of *Sharakan*s), in Festschrift in Honour of Armenuhi Drost-Abgarjan, forthcoming, Internationale Werkstücke. Deutsch-Armenische Studien, University of Halle.

Smbat Sparapet, *Datastanagirkʻ Smbat ishkhani (Gundstabli)* (Book of Judgement of Prince Smbat [the Constable]), edited by Ghltchyan, Arsēn, Ējmiatsin, 1918.

Smbatyantsʻ, Artak, *Vaweragrer Hay ekeghetsʻu patmutʻean* (Documents of the History of the Armenian Church), Vol. III, Yerevan, 1997.

Srboy Hōrn Meroy Eranelwoyn Grigori Lusaworchʻi Yachakhapatum Chaṛkʻ (Dogmatical Speeches of Our Holy Father the Blessed Gregory the Illuminator), Ējmiatsin, 1894.

St Athanasius, *Selected Works and Letters*. Edited by Schaff, Philip and Henry Wace, Peabody. MA, 1892.

Stepʻanos Ōrbēlean, *Patmutʻiwn Nahangin Sisakan* (History of the Sisakan Province), vol. I, Paris, 1859.

Tʻajiryan, Ēlisabetʻ, "Nor Jughayi S. Katarinēantsʻ Kusanatsʻ Vankʻi Ēntsayamateanĕ" (The Donation Book of the St Katarinēʼs Convent of New Julfa), *Handēs Amsōreay* 1-12, 2023, pp. 133-162.

Tashean H. Yakobos, *Vardapetutʻiwn Aṛakʻelotsʻ anvawerakan kanonatsʻ mateanĕ* (Didascalia Apostolorum: The Book of Unrecognised Canons), Vienna, 1896.

Tchilingirian, Hratch, "Historic Ordination: Tehran Prelacy of the Armenian Church Ordains Deaconess", *The Armenian Weekly*, 16 January 2018, <https://armenianweekly.com/2018/01/16/historic-ordination-tehran-diocese-armenian-church-ordains-deaconess/>, accessed on 16 January 2024.

Ter-Yakobjaneantsʻ H., *Tʻadēos Arkepiskwposi Peknazarean Arajnord Hayotsʻ Parskastani ew Hndkastani 1851-1863*, Biography of the Archbishop Tʻadēos Peknazarean, diocesan bishop of the Armenians of Persia and India 1851-1863, *Ararat*, 1906, pp. 351-362, <https://arar.sci.am/dlibra/publication/86126/edition/77895/content>, accessed 3 April 2024.

Tēr-Vardanean, Gēorg (ed.), *Mayr Mashtotsʻ* (Ritual Book), Vol. I, Book I, Surb Ejmiatsin, 2012.

The New Oxford Annotated Bible: New Revised Standard Version with the Apocrypha, edited by Michael D. Coogan. 4th ed. Oxford, 2010.

Touliatos, Diane, "Kassia", *Grove Music Online*, 2001, <https://www.oxfordmusiconline.com/grovemusic/view/10.1093/gmo/9781561592630.001.0001/omo-9781561592630-e-0000040895>, accessed on 15 January, 2024.

Tsovakan, Nersēs, "Hay Grchʻuhiner" (Armenian Women Scribes), *Sion*, IV-V, 1954, pp. 133-134.

Westphalen, Gerlinde von, *Lady Abess. Benedicta von Spiegel Politische Ordensfrau in der NS-Zeit*, 2nd ed., Münster, 2023.

Wijngaards, John (trans.), "The Barberini gr. 336 Manuscript", *Wijngaards Institute for Catholic Research*, <https://www.womendeacons.org/rite-manuscript-barberini-gr-336/≥, accessed on 23 September 2023.

Wijngaards, John (trans.), "The Thirty Canons of the Holy and Fourth Council of Chalcedon", *Wijngaards Institute for Catholic Research*, <https://www.womendeacons.org/minwest-council-of-calcedon-451ad/>, accessed on 15 January 2024.

Yardemian, Dadjad (trans.), "Niwtʻer hay vanakanutʻean patmutʻean" (Sources for the History of Armenian Monasticism), *Bazmavēp* 1-4, 1988, pp. 212-227.

Yardemian, Dadjad (trans.), "Niwtʻer hay vanakanutʻean patmutʻean" (Sources for the History of Armenian Monasticism), *Bazmavēp* 1-4, 1989, pp. 159-164.

Yovhannēs Erznkatsʻi Pluz, "Xrat hasarakatsʻ Kʻristonēitsʻ" (Advice to Ordinary Christians), MS Matenadaran 1712.

Yovsepʻeantsʻ, Garegin, *Mkhitʻar Ayrivanetsʻi: Noragyut ardzanagrutʻiwn ew erker* (Mkhitʻar Ayrivanetsʻi: Newly Discovered Inscription and Works), Jerusalem, 1931.

Zakarian, David, *Women, Too, Were Blessed: The Portrayal of Women in Early Christian Armenian Texts*, Leiden, 2021.

Zeller, Franz (trans.), *Die Apostolischen Väter*, Bibliothek der Kirchenväter, 1. Reihe, Band 35, München, 1918.

Zernov, Nicolas, "The Western Dispersion of the Armenian Church", *The Church Quarterly Review* 129, 1939, pp. 251-266.

Zernov, Nicolas (ed.), *Na Perelome: Tri Pokoleniia Odnoi Moskovskoi Semʼi (Semeynaia Khronika Zernovykh) (1812-1921)* (At the Breaking Point: Three Generations of One Moscow Family (The Family Chronicle of the Zernovs) [1812-1921]), Paris, 1970.

Zięba, Andrzej A. (ed.), *Niewiasty z Pastorałami: Portrety Ksień Klasztoru Benedyktynek Ormiańskich we Lwowie: Historia, Konteksty, Konserwacja*, Kraków, 2022.

Index

STUDIA OECUMENICA FRIBURGENSIA

113 Abel H. MANOUKIAN: The Deaconesses of the Armenian Church. Translated by David Zacharian. 189 p., 2024.

112 Adrian F. CRACIUN / André LOSSKY / Thomas POTT (éd.): Homme et femme il les créa: la place des femmes dans la liturgie. Actes de la 67e Semaine d'études liturgiques. Institut Saint-Serge, Paris, 6-9 juillet 2021 (SÉtL 67). 339 p., 2024.

111 Ciprian SAVA-POPA: Les limites de l'Église selon le concile Vatican II. Un regard orthodoxe sur un développement catholique. 431 p., 2024.

110 Nathan HOPPE: Fostering Local Eucharistic Communities. A Biblical, Historical, and Theological Reflection Inspired by Missionary Service in Albania. 325 p., 2023.

109 Stefan CONSTANTINESCU: *Visitatio Verbi* dans les Sermons *In Cantica* de Saint Bernard de Clairvaux. 343 p., 2022.

108 Oliver DÜRR: Homo Novus. Vollendlichkeit im Zeitalter des Transhumanismus (Ebook PDF). 580 S., 2021.

107 Walter DÜRR / Margareta GRUBER / Nicolas MATTER / Karl PINGGERA (Hg.): Erneuerung als Gabe und aufgabe. Beiträge zur Zukunft von Theologie und Kirche (G&G 11). 470 S., 2021.

106 Herwig ALDENHOVEN: Lex orandi – lex credendi. Beiträge zur liturgischen und systematischen Theologie in altkatholischer Tradition, hg. von Urs von Arx. VI + 453 S., 2021.

105 Oliver DÜRR / Ralph KUNZ / Andreas STEINGRUBER (Hg.): Wachet und betet. Mystik, Spiritualität und Gebet in Zeiten politischer und gesellschaftlicher Unruhe (G&G 10). 413 S., 2021.

104 Adrian Florentin CRACIUN / André LOSSKY / Thomas POTT (éd.): Liturgies de pèlerinages (SÉtL 66). 294 p., 2020.

103 Dom Cyril Pasquier: Approches du millénium. Et si Irénée de Lyon avait raison ? XXI + 808 p., 2021.

102 Arnold STEINER: Geistliche Begleitung im Protestantismus: Jean-Daniel Benoît. 108 S., 2020.

101 Hitomi OMATA RAPPO: Des Indes lointaines aux scènes des collèges. Les reflets des martyrs de la mission japonaise en Europe (XVIe-XVIIIe siècle). 598 p., 2020.

100 Theologie in weltkirchlicher Verantwortung. Die Dokumente der Internationalen Theologischen Kommission (1969-2020), hg. von Barbara Hallensleben. 1016 S., 2022.

99 Antoine ARJAKOVSKY / Barbara HALLENSLEBEN (éd.): Le Concile de Florence (1438/39) – une relecture œcuménique. 320 p., 2021.